The
Tina
Turner
Experience

The
Tina
Turner
Experience

Chris Welch

Virgin

This revised edition published in 1994 by
Virgin Books
an imprint of Virgin Publishing Ltd
332 Ladbroke Grove
London W10 5AH

First published in Great Britain in 1986 as *Take You Higher:
the Tina Turner Experience* by W.H. Allen & Co. PLC

A catalogue record for this book is available from the British Library.

ISBN 0 86369 816 6

Typeset by Phoenix Photosetting, Chatham, Kent
Printed and bound in Great Britain by Scotprint Ltd.

Every effort has been made to trace the copyright holders for the photographs
included. Any omissions or misattributions of copyright brought to the attention
of Virgin Publishing will be corrected in future editions.

The author wishes to thank the following for their help and
assistance: Bernard Doherty of Laister Dickson Ltd, Mal
Peachey, Geoff Brown, Cliff White and Jimmy Thomas.

Photograph on previous page courtesy of Laister Dickson Ltd

Contents

'Are You
Ready
For Me'?

'Are You Ready For Me'?

*I*N JANUARY 1991 Phil Spector, the producer who created one of the most dramatic pop records of all time, *River Deep Mountain High*, paid tribute to the remarkable woman who had breathed life and soul into his 1966 classic. Spector was representing the long defunct duo of Ike and Tina Turner on their induction into the Rock'n'Roll Hall of Fame. At the ceremony held at the New York Waldorf-Astoria, Spector said of Tina Turner: 'She is the closest thing to a diamond I have ever seen. She has roughness, she shines, she's bright and most of all she's priceless. And she did not receive the recognition that was due her until much too late in life.' Spector's words reflected the pangs of guilt felt by a record industry that had stepped aside when one of their number needed

help. After all, Tina had herself inducted Phil Spector into that
same Hall of Fame back in January 1989, when she was already a
legend. Her generous spirit ensures she will always remember
those who have helped her in the past.

It has been a long hard road for Tina Turner, and success,
when it came, was all the sweeter.

It was in the mid-Eighties that the world finally bestowed
megastardom on pop's most powerful singer and potent sex
symbol. Hit albums, starting with 1984's *Private Dancer*, chart

*Photograph by Laister
Jackson Ltd)*

topping singles, new audiences, massive tours, movie roles and
Grammy Awards all came in a breath-taking rush.

By 1985, the girl who had picked cotton as a child and grown
up singing in church had become an international celebrity. Her
pictures graced the covers of glossy magazines and her records
swamped radio and TV. Besides industry figures like Spector,
pop's royalty – David Bowie, Mick Jagger, Rod Stewart and Elton
John – all came to pay homage.

11

It was more than ballyhoo. It was a victory celebration and a form of penance for a star who had more than earned her title 'the hardest working woman in show business.'

There had been heartbreak and hardship along the way. There had been many peaks in her career, but there had also been dark days when she was taken for granted, ignored, or even worse, beaten and subjected to humiliation and cruelty.

Not that Tina, in her years of triumph, showed any signs of bitterness. She was just glad and proud to have won her self-respect, and her right to work. These things were more important than gold records and industry awards, although they represented visible signs of success.

Pop culture is littered with 'heroes'. Turner is one of the few who deserves the appellation. Her story, as dramatic as any Hollywood movie, eventually became the subject of a film, *What's Love Got To Do With It*, a critical and box office success in the summer of 1993. Starring Angela Bassett as Tina, it revealed the brutality the singer had suffered during her marriage to guitarist and band leader Ike Turner. It also celebrated her life in music with great spirit and panache. Well acted and with a superb soundtrack, it was one of the most powerful and authentic films of its genre.

Tina had been asked to play herself in films before, but she had always declined. She explained that she had lived the part: 'I don't need to act it!'

For much of her early career she had been chained to the man who first made her, and then almost broke her. It was Ike Turner who gave Tina her stage name and created the Ike and Tina Turner Revue, complete with the Ikettes vocal group, and backing band The Kings of Rhythm.

At a time when Ike and Tina were as close as Torvill and Dean, their show was hailed as the most exciting of its day. One early review of their act quickly spotted the potential of the singer and commented: 'Out front, the spotlight and the eyes of the audience hug Tina Turner, funky and beautiful, the embodiment of volatile sexuality. Her husky voice tailors the lyrics of a song to fit as closely as her low-necked dress.'

As far as her fans were concerned, the Tina Turner Experience was always about the power of her voice, the emotional content of her songs and her sexy image. The harsh facts of her personal life, as they were gradually revealed, shocked and dismayed the public and music business alike. Although the publicity has gained her

Tina poses for top rock photographer Paul Cox in a London session which produced some super shots (*Paul Cox/LFI*)

new respect and sympathy, the essence of her appeal still lies in her ability to entertain, to raise the spirits *and* the pulse rate. Like all great performers, she has the quality to appear both strong and vulnerable. A spitting sex kitten waiting to be tamed, a dominant leather-clad mistress of the revels, or strutting vamp . . . there is no end to the sexual fantasies she can arouse. But then the slim figure laughs raucously, whoops and sings in a voice that says: 'If you believe all this stuff then you must be crazy!'

Tina struts her stuff with pride. Give her a stage and a band and she'll explode. As she always has. Right from tiny, sweaty clubs in the Sixties, through the disco Seventies, into the video Eighties and CD Nineties.

Behind the sexual charisma, explosive wigs and sensual outfits, is a smart, experienced, witty woman, immensely charming and composed. Hers is a dignity that comes as a response to crudeness and violence. All that has happened in her life has formed her personality and shaped her career. She acknowledges this, but Tina prefers to look forward, not backwards. She has no regrets, only enthusiasm for an expanding future and new challenges.

The fans acquired during her third decade on the road are privy to an artist who long ago honed and perfected her craft. The raw power, stemming from gospel, blues and soul roots, influenced male artists like Ray Charles rather than women singers, has not diminished, even though Tina has learned to smooth out the rough edges.

In Tina Turner, audiences found everything that was lacking in white rock performers like Rod Stewart and Mick Jagger who so desperately wanted to emulate the soul and raunchy sex appeal of black artists. However, the tide of influence has not been an entirely one way affair. Jagger took his dance cues from Tina, but his enthusiasm and encouragement in return lifted her fortunes on several crucial occasions.

She and her backing band were invited to accompany The Rolling Stones on a sell-out American tour in the early Eighties, which gave her much needed exposure. During the nightly shows, Tina became the first woman to duet with Jagger, on a version of the Stones' *Honky Tonk Women*. Audiences were surprised and impressed by the spectacle of an artist who was in danger of being forgotten. Instead of presenting a ghostly reminder of the Sixties, a performer well past her peak, Tina bounced back with all her energy intact, with new songs and a fresh competitive image.

Hand clappin', foot stompin' (*David Redfern*)

14

It was with help from new-found British friends that Tina rampaged through the world's charts with *Let's Stay Together*, a cut from her sensational *Private Dancer* album, recorded in England. Musicians on the album included guitarists Jeff Beck and Dire Straits' Mark Knopfler, who wrote the title track. It marked a turning point in her career. In 1982, the year of The Stones' tour, the British recording group Heaven 17 asked Tina to sing one song, *Ball Of Confusion*, on a compilation album. This led to Heaven 17's Craig Marsh and Martyn Ware producing *Let's Stay Together*, and the rest of the album cuts on *Private Dancer*.

The single sold a million copies world-wide. This was followed by the phenomenal success of another fine song from the album, *What's Love Got To Do With It*, written by Terry Britten and Graham Lyle. With its haunting, tremulous refrain, the song virtually became Tina's anthem, and it earned her a brace of coveted Grammy Awards in February 1985.

At the Los Angeles Shrine Auditorium Awards ceremony, Tina learned that *What's Love Got To Do With It* had been voted Record of the Year, and Song of the Year; she won Best Pop Vocal Performance (Female), for the same song, and Best Rock Vocal Performance (Female) for *Better Be Good To Me*. When Tina was called up to accept her awards she later admitted that her legs were shaking and 'even the bottom lip was trembling. It was a bit of a shock'. She took the sudden deluge of awards in her stride. 'I think it was time. I don't have too much time left! I had a few cycles to go through, a few things to learn. I had to work on my own. I had to really find what I could do.'

While she enjoyed unprecedented record success, it was out on tour that the full force of her personality was unleashed. 'Are you ready for me? Are you sure?' she laughed, during a trek around Europe in late 1983 and again in 1985. Her show was dynamite. Her tiger-like roars on The Who's *Acid Queen* and *Nutbush City Limits* made strong men quake, while her outfits drove them wild. She might appear in a flimsy cave girl outfit of torn skins that complemented her ash blonde hair. Or she would slip into a leather skirt or tight denim dungarees. Along the way, she would tease and taunt and laugh and make provocative gestures.

The wild woman of rock
(*Barry Plummer*)

Tina's way was always to attack an audience at full throttle. And she dipped cheerfully into the library of white rock music, in search of a song that would provide the right vehicle for her voice and get the people off their seats.

And so in the early Eighties she was still belting through the Beatles' *Get Back*, Creedence Clearwater's *Proud Mary* and even the Chris Farlowe hit *Out Of Time*. She also regularly featured *River Deep Mountain High* in a show which came complete with a powerhouse backing band, special lighting and go-go dancers. Her sell out *Private Dancer* tour began in America in July 1984 and took her from coast-to-coast and then on to fifteen other countries, ending with British dates in March 1985. In the midst of it all, Tina had to interrupt the European dates to fly to Los Angeles to pick up her Grammy Awards.

I Can't Stand The Rain, was high in the charts when she came to Britain and demand for tickets was enormous. She played four nights at Wembley Arena and two at the massive Birmingham National Exhibition Centre. She inspired paeans of praise from the normally jaded British music press. A review by Debbie Kirby in *Black Echoes* of Tina's Wembley shows summed up the feelings of aficionados. 'I don't care that Tina Turner is now considered to be the property of the rockworld. Nor do I care that she is 46 and wears a silly wig. What I do care about is that she is one of the world's best entertainers and can still sing like you never heard anyone singing before . . . I swear that every man in the place wanted her and every woman wanted to be her.'

Britain was in the grip of 'Tina mania'. She was dubbed 'Super Gran', and 'the uncrowned queen of jungle love'. Such soubriquets were perhaps an improvement on the time when she was called 'a female Mick Jagger', or 'a lioness on heat'.

Her repertoire reflected her love of songs that showcased her passionate energy. *Let's Pretend We're Married, I Might Have Been Queen, I Can't Stand The Rain, Better Be Good To Me*, and *Private Dancer* were among the highlights, along with *Let's Stay Together*, *Help, Steel Claw* and *Proud Mary*. Canadian singer and guitarist Bryan Adams supported her on that tour and came on stage to duet with Tina on *It's Only Love*, a song recorded in Canada and featured on Adams' solo album. Bryan was one of many male rockers who enjoyed the fun of working with her. While playing London's vast Wembley Arena, she was thrilled when Elton John came on stage to present her with a bouquet of flowers and sang a duet with her on Bruce Springsteen's *Dancing In The Dark*. It was like a re-run of a duet at the Ritz in New York, when Tina joined Rod Stewart to sing his big hit *Hot Legs*. Everybody wanted to get up and jam with Tina and share in some of her radiant energy.

There were times when she just wanted to get away from it all,

Peter Jamieson, MD of EMI, presents Tina with a silver disc for UK sales of 250,000 copies of *Let's Stay Together* at a party after her show at the Venue, London, December 1983

18

Armed with success.
Tina at a London dinner
in her honour, where she
was presented with gold
and silver discs for
Private Dancer and a
silver disc for the single
*What's Love Got To Do
With It*, October 1984

to hide with friends in a restaurant over a Chinese meal, to skip the big showbiz parties and be herself, a mother of four sons, just working to earn a living. No one, not even Tina Turner, can sustain the role of being a full-time sex bomb. As she tried to explain: 'I'm quite a domestic person, down to earth, with a massive sense of humour. I love to laugh. I'm not a drab person, but it's impossible for me to be the same on and off the stage. I don't use drugs, booze or anything. I have never left the reality of life.'

The 1985 British tour ended with yet another historic duet. David Bowie appeared on stage at the Birmingham NEC to sing *Tonight* with Tina, and a rousing chorus of his 1983 No. 1 hit *Let's Dance*. Said David: 'Standing next to her up there was the hottest place in the universe.'

With such a gruelling work load, it was possible to imagine that Turner would grow bored or exhausted, but she never seemed to lose her zest and enthusiam. 'I love touring,' said Tina. 'I particularly love travelling in Europe, seeing the differences in lifestyles and traditions from the American way of life. If I'm at home for a month, I'm ready to tour again. It is a lot of work and it's also very glamourous. But I never seem to get enough rest.'

Showbiz glamour does tend to fade when an artist has been on the road for as long as Tina. It was certainly a lot more unpredictable in the old days, when bullets whistled by and promoters made off with the takings. Despite the adoration heaped on her nightly, touring in the New Age of Tina had become a well organised, but essentially mundane chore. Tina explained how she coped with her business life style: 'We tour by bus. It's more relaxing for me, and I can see a lot of the countryside as well. I'm really fed up with flying. You get on a 'plane and by the time you sit down, it's time to get off. Then you gotta go through customs and collect your baggage . . . it's a hassle. I'm always working and I like to keep my band busy. This is my living, and I'm not the type of person to sit back and do nothing. I get too restless too quickly! I'm a master of my work. I've been entertaining all my life. I am true to my profession and I owe my audiences the best. They know I have my own style and this is what they come to see. I have a natural energy and once I get on stage I'm in a whole different world. I won't let up because it is me and I ain't gonna change now.'

As the tide of success has turned her way, she has often thought what she might do if she didn't have to go on stage every night.

'If I wasn't an entertainer, then I could do something else creative. For instance, maybe in cosmetics, doing people's hair or even being a decorator. I've always decorated my own homes. If it all ended for me tomorrow, I could certainly earn a living.' Doubtless she was joking, like the time she told a reporter that her ambition was 'to be a fireman'.

But during 1985 there were signs that there was another career waiting for her, if the time came when she had to quit the road. It seemed her potential as an actress was being tapped at last. Her first major dramatic role was in *Mad Max: Beyond Thunderdome*, the third in a series of cult movies. In it she played Aunt Entity, the ruler of a post-Apocalypse city called Bartertown, where all disputes were settled by hand-to-hand combat. This resulted in such ferocious duels between Mel 'Max' Gibson and Tina that some thought the fourth in the series should be called *Mad Tina*.

Accompanying the movie was a soundtrack album with two songs featuring Tina, *We Don't Need Another Hero*, written by Terry Britten, and *One Of The Living*. Tina had already had one film role as the Acid Queen in Ken Russell's epic version of The Who's *Tommy*. Many thought her appearance, emoting her way through the Pete Townshend song, was the best part of an over-the-top movie. All the more astonishing then that Tina, capable of so much as a performer, singer and actress should have been so shamefully ignored and neglected in the lean years that separated the two key phases of her life.

But where there is neglect, there is usually someone, somewhere, ready to lend a hand, as long as the subject shows a willingness to co-operate. In Tina's case it was a combined effort: a story of people having faith when others turned their backs and of entrepreneurs pitting their skill and enthusiasm towards rebuilding a shattered career, when many promoters wouldn't even offer a booking. Tina herself now tends to dismiss her post-Ike and Tina struggles fairly lightly. Explaining why it took her nearly eight years, she says: 'The first four years it was just getting promoters to book me!'

The key was finding the right management. In this she was supremely successful. In 1979 she met and obtained the services of a 33-year-old Australian, Roger Davies. Having escaped from the clutches of a Svengali, she found herself under the protection of a knight crusader. The result was, as Tina put it: 'I was able to do everything I wanted to do, to get back to the right rock circuit and into the press . . . to bring myself back to life.'

Tina and megastar Dav Bowie backstage at Birmingham after they had sung *Tonight* together. Said Tina: 'Tonight has got to be one of the highlights of my life.' Saturday 23 March 1985 (*Syndicatio International*)

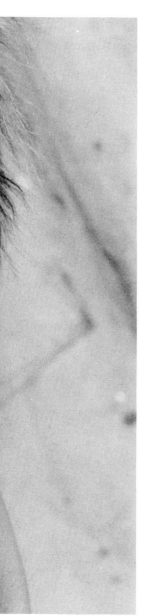

In the wake of *Private Dancer*, the album that Davies helped secure, life was good. And there were many more hit albums to come. *Break Every Rule* (1986), *Foreign Affair* (1989), *Simply The Best* (1991), and *What's Love Got To Do With It* (1993) all sold millions.

Yet the road to quadruple platinum albums, sell out stadium concerts, block buster movies and Grammy Awards, began long ago in the strangest location, with a young girl bearing the most unlikely name . . .

Older, wiser and more beautiful – Tina in 1985
(*Paul Cox/LFI*)

'I Didn't
Know
You
Could
Sing'

'I Didn't Know You Could Sing'

*T*HE GIRL who became an international star was born Anna Mae Bullock, in Brownsville, Tennessee, some fifty miles north of Memphis. Her birthdate is usually given as 26 November 1939. Her mother Zelma gave birth to her at the Haywood Memorial hospital. She was raised in the township of Flatbush, celebrated in song as Nutbush. Her father, Floyd Richard Bullock, was a farm manager and 'share cropper' who worked on a white-owned plantation. As children, Anna Mae and her older sister Alline helped pick cotton and strawberries. Their father, always called Richard, was a Deacon at the local Baptist Church and ensured his family attended church regularly.

Zelma had a powerful voice and sang in the Knoxville Baptist Church choir. Part black and part Cherokee Indian, Zelma had the high cheekbones inherited by Anna which gave her such a dramatic appearance. She also inherited her mother's voice, which she was able to show off both in the church choir and while singing opera at school.

Although they lived in the South and Mr Bullock worked in the classic circumstances of many black Americans who hadn't migrated to the big cities, they weren't particularly poor or unhappy. They lived in a comfortable house, got on with their white neighbours and says Tina: 'We always had nice furniture.' The girls had their own bedroom, separate from their parents, and the family owned livestock which included pigs and goats.

Tina attended a small school which had only two classrooms, and didn't enjoy lessons. She preferred the summer picnics, where there was live music, often provided by a trombone player known as Bootsy Whitelaw, who was accompanied by a drummer. The two-man band made some great sounds in the swing, jump blues style of the Forties, and everyone encouraged Anna Mae to get up and sing with 'Mr Bootsy'.

As well as singing swing at picnics, and later hot gospel in church, Anna began to absorb the blues music she heard regularly on the local black radio stations. She loved the famous 'King Biscuit Hour', a show sponsored by the biscuit company and hosted by Sonny Boy Williamson. Listening to him made her think she might be able to pursue a career as a singer, rather than pickin' cotton.

The only stumbling block to an otherwise happy childhood was the fact that Tina's parents were constantly arguing. In their teens, both Anna Mae and Alline were deserted by their mother and later their father, and put into the care of relatives. When Richard and Zelma moved to Knoxville to work at a Government atomic plant, Anna Mae was sent to stay with her grandmother, Roxanna Bullock. Anna later moved to Knoxville, either staying with her parents for short spells or with family friends. 'My parents never got along,' says Tina. 'My mother was always leaving him and going to my grandmother's house. When my mother left, it left me very lonely and sad for a long time. I had to think about what I could do – *not* pick cotton!'

In Knoxville, the young Anna Mae was exposed to the excitement of 'holy roller' church services where there was much hand clapping and dancing in the aisles, all of which would be an obvious influence on her future career.

She heard a different kind of music blaring out from back street bars and juke joints in the rougher parts of town in nearby Ripley. Rhythm & Blues was the music of black Americans in the early

Gift wrapped: Hollywood-style publicity shot

30

32

Fifties; it was eventually espoused by white audiences as Rock'n'Roll. There was little crossover in pop music, and radio stations, like buses, were segregated. The blues was even referred to as 'race music' and confined to its own charts. And yet Rock'n'Roll, when it burst upon an astonished world in 1954, was based on the music that black choirs, bands and vocal groups had been playing for years.

Black artists had transformed the old country blues and made the music more acceptable to audiences in the northern cities. Local radio stations, and the 'chitlin' circuit' of clubs provided a framework within which black bands could grow and develop. There was plenty of work and a great outpouring of music. Black audiences demanded music that suited their aspirations and provided solid, hip entertainment.

Rhythm & Blues was a term that covered a multitude of styles, from frenetic jump music with jazz influenced horns, to ballads delivered by guitars and vocal harmony groups. While the big record companies stuck to swing bands and crooners, the new market was catered for by small independent record companies, which at least gave hope and exposure to up and coming artists, even if there was usually a lack of hard cash.

Anna Mae Bullock particularly admired 'King of the Blues' guitarist B.B. King, who was working out of Memphis, the city where Elvis Presley, Jerry Lee Lewis and Carl Perkins began the process of fusing Country and Western music with R&B.

This was the time when black Americans began to demand greater freedom within society. Music had always been a meeting point between black and white cultures in America. Entertainers and their fans were the ones most likely to mix and break down the barriers. There was little need to politicise the lyrics or sing protest songs. The sheer energy, style and drive of the music was in itself an expression of new found pride and confidence. All these factors would influence the future music and career of Tina Turner.

Zelma and Richard's marital problems culminated with their final separation in 1954. Anna Mae was sixteen when she and Alline moved with their mother from Knoxville, Tennessee, to St Louis, Missouri. There was plenty of musical action in the city, and Anna began hanging out at the local blues clubs, hoping that maybe some night, someone would ask her to get up and sing, just like they had at the picnics and parties back home. Big sister Alline started going to the Club Manhattan in East St Louis. It was a smart place where the clientèle wore sharp suits, pretty dresses and lots of jewellery.

Hi fellas – this is how you do The Popcorn

OVERLEAF: Where are they now? The whole shebang, circa 1963

33

Anna was seventeen years old when she was taken to the club one night to see a band led by one of the most respected musicians in St Louis, The Kings of Rhythm. That musician was the charismatic Ike Turner.

She was intrigued by the slim, good-looking dude who played organ and guitar, and had a mean, smouldering look in his eyes. He was surrounded by beautiful women who seemed to come running whenever he called. She may have felt a gawky teenager, even a country hick, but she knew there was a way to attract his attention. She approached him. Could she sit in with the Kings of Rhythm and sing a couple of numbers? Ike wasn't too keen. He was mostly concerned with such problems as how to extricate himself from a half-dozen female admirers who were all paying calls at the same time. He'd stay on stage, even when the band took a break, and play around with the Hammond organ. Finally he'd call up his wife to get him out of the club.

Then one night, tired of hanging around waiting to be asked, Tina jumped on stage while Ike was sitting at the organ, grabbed the microphone and began singing one of her favourite B.B. King songs. Her voice roared around the club and customers came running to the stage to find out who was singing. The song over, Ike came down from the stage, looked at Tina somewhat shyly, and in surprised tones said: 'I didn't know you could *really* sing.'

Annie later recalled the events that led to her meeting Ike. 'I was going to nightclubs with my sister. Ike was working at one that we used to go to all the time. Well, I used to ask him to let me sing. He'd say "Okay," but never call me to the stage.

'One night he was playing organ and the drummer put a microphone in front of my sister for her to sing. She said "No!" so that's when I took the mike and started singing. Ike was shocked! When he finished one tune, he called me on stage. I did several numbers with them that night. Later I joined the group.'

Ike was born Izear Luster Turner, in Clarksdale, Mississippi, on 5 November, 1931. He was the son of a preacher, and began making music from the age of six. His first instrument was the piano. Says Ike: 'I played on an old piano in a church lady's house. She would let me play if I cut wood for her in return. At that time, I didn't really know what a piano was. All I knew was that when I pushed down on the keys it made a sound I liked.'

After picking out a few notes to such songs as *Blues In The Night* Ike begged his mother to buy him his own piano. 'When school was out that year I came home with my report card full of good

grades. I walked in the house and there it was. A new piano. She said it was all mine.'

Ike taught himself, but the famed pianist Pinetop Perkins (not Pinetop Smith), showed him how to play the rolling left-hand boogie woogie beat. He started playing at school and formed a band called the Tophatters, with his schoolfriend Raymond Hill on saxophone. Aged only sixteen, the go-getting young Turner got himself a job as a DJ and standby studio musician on the local Clarksdale radio station. The next step was to put together his own fully professional band, which became known as 'the Kings of Rhythm' – the first in a long line of such aggregations.

By the age of twenty in 1951 Ike and the Kings of Rhythm went to Memphis to start recording. Under the supervision of producer Sam Phillips in a Memphis studio, the band cut a number called *Rocket 88*. Released on the Chess label it became a smash hit. Ike played boogie piano, while Jackie Brenston sang and played saxophone. The performance was so exciting it inspired a country and western band leader called Bill Haley to change his musical direction, and cover the song himself.

Unfortunately the unexpected hit led to a bust-up which hurt Ike badly and may have turned him into a much harder, more cynical character. Jackie Brenston felt that his singing and input had made the record, so he left and took the band with him. Ike's own song, cut on the same day as *Rocket 88* and released as a single *Heartbroken And Worried* coupled with *I'm Lonesome Baby* was a flop. He rarely sang on record again.

Nevertheless Sam Phillips, who later went on to record Elvis Presley, could see that Ike Turner had talent and was adept at finding good performers, even if he wasn't so hot at holding on to them. Phillips employed Turner as a talent scout and producer. Ike would bring in talent for labels like Modern and Sun. One of his major discoveries was bluesman Howlin' Wolf. He also helped B.B. King, Bobby Bland and Elmore James.

Ike became a powerful, respected figure in the years before he met up with Anna Mae Bullock in St Louis. So much so that even the errant Jackie Brenston and Raymond Hill returned to help form the next Kings of Rhythm.

In 1958 Ike cut a single for the Tune Town label called *Boxtop* which featured Ike together for the first time with Little Ann, who was of course, Annie Mae Bullock. Ike looked back on his early efforts with a mixture of chagrin and pride. '*Rocket 88* was a big financial score . . . but some dude at the record company beat me, and I only got forty dollars for writing, producing and recording it.

Tina meets Cher in a TV chat show

36

38

After that I took the Kings on the road, doing shows with Howlin'
Wolf and B.B. King. Somehow I ended up in St Louis and was
playing at this nightclub, and through unique circumstances, I met
Annie Bullock . . . the future Tina Turner!'

The lives of the musicians, constantly on the road, working all
hours, often until four in the morning, led to all kinds of
entanglements and complications. Ike had a common-law wife and
two sons. He had made the move to East St Louis in 1956 and
lived with his family in a large three-storey house. He had early on
acquired a taste for flashy living, and believed in the motto 'if you
got it, flaunt it'. But his extravagances required frequent injections
of cash so he worked long hours. In the early part of the evening
he booked his band to play at the Club Imperial, then on to the
Club D'Lisa, winding up at the Club Manhattan, playing the
rocking blues until sun-up.

As Annie Mae became part of the band, Ike kept his distance
and looked after her more like a brother or a father figure. He was
pleased with his discovery and wanted to make her a star.

He bought her special stage clothes, jewellery, even a padded
bra. She rode around in Ike's latest mad passion, a pink Fleetwood
Cadillac. 'I felt like I was rich, and it felt good!' she chuckled.
Romantically she was drawn, not to Ike, but to his sax player
Raymond Hill. Not long after leaving high school, Annie became
pregnant by Raymond and they had a son, named Raymond Craig.
There was no time for rest or motherhood. Tina was soon back on
the road with the band, earning up to twenty dollars a night.

Then Ike decided to try his luck in the recording studios again.
This time he wanted to make a demo of a song he'd written called
A Fool In Love. He intended it to be sung by Art Lassiter, one of
the Kings of Rhythm. But after a row with Ike over some detail of
band affairs, Lassiter failed to turn up. Annie was given her
chance to sing instead. Her voice ripped through the song, and
when the record company heard it, they flipped. It was released by
the Sue label and was an immediate hit. It got to number
twenty-seven in America's pop chart, and number two in the more
specialized R&B chart. The 'demo' became the smash hit of 1960.

Ike realized he couldn't call the new partnership Turner and
Bullock, which would have sounded like a firm of plumbers. He
had to come up with something more hip to suit the record
company and to flow off the tongues of disc jockeys and record
buyers.

Bullock would have to go. Without consulting Annie Mae, he
came up with the name Tina, inspired by a jungle queen from a

Hold on baby

long forgotten film serial. 'Ike and Tina Turner' sounded great. Yet it suggested they were married, which they weren't and 'Tina' resented having her name changed without her permission. With a record on the charts already credited to the new act, Tina was in no position to start fighting back. She was also ill. Just as *A Fool In Love* zoomed upwards, she went down with a severe bout of yellow jaundice, probably brought on by all the irregular hours and endless travelling.

Ike wasn't pleased. He dragged her from her sickbed and set her off on the road. The pattern was formed. Tina was obviously going to be a source of hits and a star attraction on the road. She wanted to go to pleasure island, but the puppetmaster was going to pull the strings.

Gradually, the relationship between Ike and Tina ceased to be strictly platonic. Perhaps because of all his philandering, Ike had broken up with his wife, and he asked Tina if she would come with him to California, where he was due to start recording. Tina agreed. After some time on the road, with Tina singing *A Fool In Love* backed up by their new all-girl vocal group, named The Ikettes, Tina became pregnant, by Ike.

Perhaps in panic, Ike chose this moment to decide to go back to his common-law wife. But this meant loosening his grip on the sensationally sexy young singer whose talents were the key to a golden future.

Ike returned to Tina and this time proposed marriage. They went to Tijuana in Mexico, in 1962, where weddings were conducted briskly, with no questions asked. Tina was unhappy with these arrangements. They didn't seem very romantic, even though she felt affection towards Ike. Already she was beginning to wonder what she had got herself into, and began to make tentative moves to break away. But it was too late. When Ike wanted to sign them to a big record company for a lucrative deal, and his star hinted that she wanted out, he beat her up. From the outset their relationship was stormy and often violent. And yet Tina was still drawn to him. She admired him as the boss who had given her fame, money and a role in life. She had a son by Ike, and together with Ike's own offspring, and Tina's boy from the affair with Raymond Hill, there were four sons to look after. Tina was trapped.

When things were good, Ike remained charming, amusing company. He was the business brains, the composer, the band leader, and general wheeler dealer. Without him there would have been no motivation. Nothing would have happened.

Those popular recording stars – Ike & Tina! (*Pye Records Ltd*)

OVERLEAF: Chubby cheeked, sixties dolly bird (*H. Goodwin*)

40

It is possible to understand why Ike dealt with Tina the way he did. As a black American fighting his way up in a white-controlled world, there were plenty of pressures and tensions. He had to assert himself. Anyone who got in the way would have to be slapped down. The problem came when the occasional, forgivable outburst became a built-in pattern to their lives. Tina was torn between love, duty, guilt and fear. The conflict between them was evident right from the beginning and it was obvious that the pair were incompatible. But there was no one who could really help them. There are few more dangerous situations than interfering between a man and his wife, even with the best of intentions. And so the band would listen to the thumps and yells coming from the dressing room, and would shrug, wince and maybe even joke about it. Eventually 'Ike and Tina' became a working relationship, sustained by the hit records.

A Fool In Love was a devastating performance making a tremendous impact on white listeners more used to singers like Doris Day and Rosemary Clooney. In her harsh, sandpapery outbursts of wordless 'vocalese' Tina was echoing a style that went back to the Cotton Club and the Duke Ellington recordings of the Twenties. But nobody had sung with such a range of expression in that style before, and even in the lower register she added emphasis and sudden thrusts that were impressive to hear, and technically difficult to produce. Their next record *I Idolise You* was another R&B chart hit, but didn't cross-over into the white pop charts. A third single was a flop.

Their fourth single for the Sue label, was, to Ike's relief, a hit. But he didn't have much to do with it. Another team of songwriters and producers were brought in to try and rescue the situation. They were Mickey Baker and Sylvia Robinson, who had enjoyed their own hits like *Love Is Strange*. They worked up a song called *It's Gonna Work Out Fine* which had a call and response pattern, similar to the gospel routine where preacher and congregation interacted. It had been the mainstay of the blues, and incidentally had been the basis of most big band swing music.

It's Gonna Work Out Fine was strictly secular and very much a modern soul performance. It became one of the biggest hits of 1961, coupled with *Won't You Forgive Me*. Most people assumed it was Ike Turner engaging Tina in the amusing banter and cool dude responses. But it was later revealed that the deadpan dialogue came from Mickey Baker, while Sylvia played the shimmering guitar licks. The couple also wrote the song, using the pseudonym Seneca and Lee.

42

The record was billed under Ike's name, even though he wasn't even in the studio. Reaching number two in the R&B chart in the autumn of 1961, it rocketed to fourteen in the national charts. Their star status was confirmed.

The couple stayed with Sue Records until 1963 and among their other releases for the label were *Poor Fool*, *Tra La La La La*, *You Should've Treated Me Right*, (which was a chart hit in June 1962), *Please Don't Hurt Me*, and Ike's guitar instrumental, accompanied by a jumping big band, *Prancing*.

Many of the lyrics on Tina's songs during the Sue years have a strangely ironic flavour in view of later revelations. For example, on *Worried And Hurtin' Inside* she opens up with a blistering unaccompanied outburst: 'Now baby, you mean everything to me, and the last thing I'd want to do is break up with you . . .' She goes on to shout 'stop your shoving and treating me wrong!'

This wasn't one of Tina's more attractive vocal performances, but *Dear John* issued in 1966 was an extraordinary semi-spoken

Talented talons (*Barry Plummer*)

44

45

testament about 'the evilest, most rotten, lowdown man I've ever met in my whole life!' She complains about beatings and black eyes, while Ike noodles idly on the organ in the background. If she wasn't joking, it was a miracle she got away with it. However, it must have been good therapy.

Ike meanwhile was out battling with record companies. He had cause to complain. He had already experienced rip-offs and rebuffs from the earliest days. He complained: 'I wrote thirty-two hits for one firm, but I didn't know what a songwriter's royalties were. I didn't know nothing. They were sending me a hundred and fifty dollars a week which was enough to keep me happy in Mississippi but not enough for me to get away to find out what was really going on.'

Ike had also had trouble with the master tapes he had been sending to Sue, who often rejected them and sent them right back again. But they recorded five albums for Sue, none of which were released in England. Sue products were then issued in Britain on the London label, until in 1963, a British Sue label was formed. London, part of Decca Records, did however issue an album called *The Story* which included two Ike and Tina tracks *It's Gonna Work Out Fine*, and *A Fool In Love*. But neither of these tracks, issued as singles, were hits in Britain at the time.

After the Sue experience, Ike signed his outfit to a succession of record companies. He also tried to form his own label, the shortlived Sonja. Ike and Tina went on record for the Modern label, as well as Warner's subsidiary Loma. Among their hits for the latter label was *Finger Poppin'* (1965). They went back to Sue records for a while, had a spell with Kent/Modern and then signed with Ray Charles' label Tangerine, for whom they recorded an album called *Ike and Tina Turner And The Raelettes*.

In between all the recording activity, the revue kept on working on the road, Ike in his shiny suits and Tina in long dresses that gradually became shorter, until they reached above her knees.

In 1966 the show was recorded on a live album for Warner, re-issued in 1985 on the Edsel label. It was cut at the Skyliner Ballroom, Fort Worth, Texas, and at Lovall's Ballroom, Dallas, and provides a revealing insight into the styles and standards of the time. On the opening number *Finger Poppin'* which has a strong Twist beat, Tina sounds hot, bothered and somewhat strangled. In contrast, one of the singers in the band, Jimmy Thomas revealed a much more melodic voice on *Down In The Valley*. The contention in those days was that Tina was trying too hard to be regarded as a quality, legitimate singer. And there was no doubt on items like

'You're the meanest, most rotten, low down man I ever met in my whole life! . . .' (*S.K.R Photos*)

46

Good Times that she tended to present a rather rough blend of Sam Cooke and Otis Redding styles. She was still learning and needed to develop and control her talent. Once again, Tina's violent attack on *You Are My Sunshine* with Ike, contrasted rather poorly with guest singer Vanetta Fields' straightforward performance on *Having A Good Time*.

When the album was recorded, Ike and Tina Turner had become hot property in America and they were invited to appear on many top US TV shows like 'Shindig' and the long-running 'American Bandstand'. And there was no doubt, when Tina screamed at the climax of the classic Sixties' rave-up number *Twist And Shout* that complaints about her lack of finesse became rather piddling and academic!

Macho Man: Ike Turner
with faithful spouse

Cruisin'
on the
Chitlin'
Circuit

Cruisin' on the Chitlin' Circuit

*T*HE IKE and Tina Turner Revue became an exciting way of life for the singers and musicians who passed through the ranks, even for the ever-changing, often grumbling Ikettes. Among the most celebrated of a succession of girls, personally groomed by Tina for their all-singing, all-dancing role, were Bonnie Bramlett, a white girl destined for fame with Delaney and Bonnie, and P. P. Arnold, who had success as a solo artist in England.

As well as the Ikettes, the Revue sported various male singers. One of them, Jimmy Thomas, joined the band as a teenager in 1959. His rich, melodic voice was used on songs like *Down In The Valley* or on the Bobby Darin hit *Splish Splash*. He was whisked away from his home town, and found himself travelling all over

America with Ike and Tina. He drove their limousine, belting across the empty highways in the early hours of the morning, in 100 m.p.h. dashes from town to town.

Although younger than the rest, Jimmy was well versed in blues and R&B and grew up listening to the music of Big Maceo and Sonny Boy Williamson. He formed his own band when still at school and eventually got to know many of the top local musicians.

Among them was guitarist Albert King, who recommended Jimmy to Ike Turner. Jimmy was well aware of Ike's reputation and was thrilled when the call came to replace Clayton Love in the Revue.

Jimmy stayed with Ike for eight years and witnessed the arrival of Annie Mae Bullock. In 1966 Jimmy came to England with the Revue when they supported the Rolling Stones on tour. He was enamoured of the country and its thriving music scene, and later came back to settle in London with an English wife. He runs his own record label, Osceola, named after the town in Arkansas, where he was born on 20 January, 1939. Jimmy now lives in a tiny flat in Shepherds Bush, where he makes demos and writes songs like his medium-sized hit *Hang Right On In There*. He has fond memories of Tina, and talks about her with a brotherly affection that is not above the occasional note of criticism.

Surrounded by tape recorders, keyboards and guitars, he recalled those years when Tina was hailed as 'the Human Bombshell', years when the band slogged its way round the 'chitlin' circuit' before going on to enjoy its big breakthroughs, with television appearances, and tours abroad with its mentors, the Stones.

Says Jimmy: 'Albert King got me the gig with Ike and Tina Turner. He knew my family and stuff. I was still in high school and I had a little band in Osceola. Albert lived in St Louis where he knew Ike needed a new singer. Ike was the hottest thing in that part of the world, in the South and Midwest. He was like God!'

Albert, who dubbed Jimmy 'Popeye', came by one morning yelling outside Thomas' window: 'Wake up Popeye! I'm coming to take you to St Louis. No, it's not for me, it's for Ike's band!'

Says Jimmy: 'I could have died.'

Jimmy had seen Ike's band at the Imperial Club which let black artists play to white audiences. Ike had been one of the first local artists to reach the young white crowd.

Says Jimmy: 'There was a lot of competition among the bands. They really had to try hard to win over the audiences. When I joined in early 1959 I was right out of school. I was seventeen years old, very young, but old enough, if you know what I mean. You grow up pretty fast in America.'

Ike had spotted Popeye singing at the T99 club, which usually featured artists like B.B. King, Bobby Bland and Chuck Berry. 'They were all the hot blues cats. We were the local boys, struggling to start a band. I thought Ike was very underrated, the way he played guitar. He was also responsible for discovering people like Howlin' Wolf, all them blues guys. Ike used to record them all. He was also a very good boogie woogie player.'

From being a struggling newcomer, admiring the likes of Ike Turner from afar, Jimmy found himself in at the deep end. 'It was good fun. I was overawed by it all. You didn't have time to think much about it, just chase chicks and make music. We dressed smart and rode around in big Cadillac cars. We made pretty good money, but we weren't getting rich. It was only success on a local level. It was all Ike's thing, even when it became Ike and Tina Turner. The rest of us were on salaries.

'When we got a big hit, we started travelling and things really began to go! Who cared about money anyway, as long as the hotel bills were paid!'

Albert King drove Jimmy Thomas to St Louis for his first meeting with Ike. Jimmy provides a revealing insight into the way Ike and Tina and their fellow artists lived and worked in those hectic days.

'Meeting Ike was unnerving. He was my hero. He had a long Cadillac parked outside his house. It was pink and black. He also had a couple of station wagons, with his name plastered all over them. Inside his house he had a big piano and there were amplifiers all over the place, things a small town boy hadn't seen before. But I was cool. I sung while he sat down and played the piano. He said I had a nice voice, but he thought I was a bit young. His band had been mostly blues orientated, and billed as Ike Turner and the Kings of Rhythm. I wasn't a blues belter, I had a light voice. It wasn't whiskey-sodden. So it was a kind of novelty. My whole bag was rock'n'roll. Chuck Berry was my man. I could take him off and knew all his songs.'

Ike, like Berry, realized that a mass market for rock'n'roll and pop music was waiting to be exploited. Nobody wanted the old style blues any more. 'So Ike's band started to play lighter things,' recalls Jimmy. 'It could flirt with pop. I even did Bobby Darin's *Splish Splash* all that shit!'

The song was featured on one of the Ike Turner band's first TV appearances. They went out live on a show on a St Louis station,

PREVIOUS PAGE: Her man, his women (*Tom Hanley*)

What you see is what you get

TOP RIGHT: Radiating humour in the Paisley-clad sixties (*Barry Plummer*)

BOTTOM RIGHT: Mr and Mrs Music. Ike and Tina relax in a hotel lobby (*Barry Plummer*)

56

sponsored by a washing machine manufacturer.

Jimmy had to jump out of a washing machine with a towel around his waist, singing *Splish Splash* while lathered in suds. 'That was my big break. Television! The white kids loved our act and all you heard about was Ike Turner and his Kings of Rhythm.'

Mercifully the Revue cast were spared such indignities out on the road. The show was fast, hot and hip. They invariably closed the first half with a Ray Charles number called *Tell The Truth*. Says Jimmy: 'We played it way uptempo and it would always be the climax of the first show. Strobe lights would start going, girls kicking and Tina doing it.' Jimmy danced across the stage on one leg, grabbed Tina and the pair of them fell down and started screaming. It was an R&B ballet.

'We just danced. It was great. I could understand why Mick Jagger just used to stand and look at us in the wings when we came over to England for our first tour. Mick may have taken some things from us in his stage routine, but we all borrow from somebody else. I used to think I could sing like Chuck Berry. In the middle of all that you develop your own style. Mick Jagger's performance is his own. I could think of a lot of people Tina worshipped, like Ray Charles. But everybody did. James Brown taught us a lot too, plus some guys out of St Louis called the Sharpies, a soul vocal group. They were with us for a while and they taught Tina a lot of steps and routines.'

When Jimmy Thomas joined them, the band had already created a market without hit records, and Ike had a sizeable following in the mid-western cities even before the arrival of Tina. But, when Tina joined and they had their hit *A Fool In Love*, according to Jimmy they were still only reaching an R&B audience.

'We used to play the chitlin' circuit,' says Jimmy, 'which was like funny clubs stuck out in the middle of nowhere and in poverty-stricken ghetto areas.' Chitterlings, or 'chitlins' are 'the intestines of a pig prepared as a dish' according to Collins' Dictionary. The chitlin' circuit was the equivalent of the 'chicken in the basket' nightclub scene which flourished in England in the Sixties, albeit more down-market.

Recalls Jimmy: 'On the chitlin' circuit you know you are down with the dregs, but it's the place where everybody goes. Ike and Tina, James Brown, Bobby Bland, B.B. King – whoever came through town, played the chitlin' circuit. Bands then began to break out of that mould, got more popular and played the local civic auditorium which held five thousand people. James Brown

Night after night, town after town on the Chitlin' circuit (*Barry Plummer*)

58

was one of the first black artists to achieve that. He'd clean up with a big crowd and we'd be down the road playing one of them funky joints, 'cos we couldn't fill the Civic. That was the chitlin' circuit.'

At this time Ike's band had two guitarists, including Ike, a baritone and two tenor sax players, and for bigger shows they'd add a trumpet. 'We also had another guitarist to play on the band's set before the actual show.'

Showtime featured Tina, Jimmy and the Ikettes. 'Ike would pick up his guitar, tune it, come out with *Prancin'*, an instrumental, and say, "Ladies and gentlemen, it's showtime. Sit back and enjoy the Ike and Tina Revue." Sometimes I would open the show, sometimes the girls. It was a really good show, which you don't see any more. You had to get ugly to put on a show. Really screw your face up! It used to be an in-joke within the band. Ike and Tina would hit town and one of the girls in the Ikettes would give notice that she wanted to quit. We'd be quietly scouting for a replacement. We'd ask if there were any gospel girls from the local church. If one turned up and was a beautiful-looking chick, we'd say "She looks great. Bet she can't sing, man." One would come through looking like a gorilla or something. Ike would say "Hey, hire it." It would be a little game. It always worked. Sure enough, she'd chirp like a bird.'

Tina had considerable say in the hiring and firing of the Ikettes. 'Tina would do most of the scrutinizing as she'd have to train the girl in the steps. Ike would check if she looked presentable on stage. The whole idea was action. That's why they all wore wigs, popping their heads. It wasn't just an illusion though, we were all working our asses off! The wigs and short dresses were to emphasize the action. Tina would say, "Well she's all right but she can't dance too good." Mostly the three of us did the checking out.'

Later various Ikettes would claim the Turners were hard bosses, mean and selfish, with a system of fines for misdemeanours like laddering a stocking or laughing too loud at private jokes. Most of the girls left because of the army style training and discipline, others simply to get married.

Jimmy had no complaints. 'Ike was all right. I can understand why a lot of people criticized him for being a hard guy to work for. But I didn't think so, not at all. I suppose I was brainwashed into thinking the way he thought. He had proven himself to be right so often, I trusted his judgement. Sometimes I felt he was harsh on people. But without his domineering strength, it would all have fallen apart.'

PREVIOUS PAGE: Hands, knees and boomps-a-daisy (*S.K.R. Photos*)

Thomas feels Ike had the ability to bring out the best in people. 'People might come in with no confidence, but they did have ability. Tina became a totally different person after Ike met her. She had the voice and the ability to sing, but there was a lot of competition on stage, within the group. In the dressing room, we'd say, "I'm gonna kick your ass tonight!"'

'She was never shy. Ike was more shy. She'd come off stage, dripping in sweat saying "I got 'em, I killed 'em! Follow that!" If the other local bands were cookin' we had to try and upgrade our performance. The girls competed among themselves on stage even though we were all working as a unit. The guys, me included, were all competing with each other.'

There was heavy competition, too, between Ike and the other stars, like James Brown. If James had a diamond ring with so many carats, Ike would try and beat him and get one bigger. James was reported to have a Cadillac covered in leather, from the front grille to the back bumper. Ike got a car striped like a Zebra.

Jimmy recalls Tina's arrival in the band and how she was given her new name. 'We thought the name up, Ike and myself. We thought: "Hell, we can't go out under the name of Annie Mae Bullock. Ha, ha!" I didn't see what was wrong with Little Ann, but Ike said, "No, the name must change. Gotta make it snappy. Ike and Annie Mae? No, no!" He had bad experiences with other singers, like Clayton Love, who had become famous in their own right and quit the band, leaving him in the lurch. He got tired of this, so it became Ike Turner and the Kings of Rhythm. If you wanted to build yourself up, you could do it outside. He got smart about that. So he kept his name on everything. He was always making records, using different names. He felt cheated when guys left his group, even though the reason they left in the first place was because *they* felt cheated.

'He wanted to change Annie Mae to Tina to safeguard his own control over the situation. He gave her his name, and there's no way she would have stuck it as long as she did otherwise.

'A lot of times, in private conversations with Tina, away from Ike, she confided in me, and expressed her feelings about him. She ran away a couple of times. It wasn't very pleasant when he caught up with her, y'know what I mean?'

A Fool In Love cemented the business relationship and necessitated the name change. 'If she'd had her own name there wouldn't have been a thing Ike could have done about anything, legally. So he was thinking ahead when he gave her that name. We sat up all night thinking. "What the hell are we gonna call her?

How are we gonna name the band? It can't be Ike and the Kings of Rhythm any more. We got a girl singing lead now, and people will wanna know who she is, her voice is so unusual."

'This was when Ike recorded *A Fool In Love* and Art Lassiter didn't turn up for the session. Art sang a lot like Ray Charles, and Tina could kind of imitate that as a girl. She had studied Art's phrasing enough to know how to sing the song. So Ike just changed the key in the studio and she sang it. It was her big chance. When it got on the radio everybody was crazy about it. The top DJs said it was gonna be a hit.

'So we sat up with this problem. What are we gonna call the act? Ike Turner? Impossible. That's where Johnny Otis made a mistake. He had a lot of artists in his band but it was always the Johnny Otis Show. Ike didn't want to be *that* unfair.

'He compromised, kept Turner and dreamt up something snappy to go with Ike. It would be "Ike and Something Turner" – a nice rhythmic thing that would roll off the tongue of the DJs.'

Names were written down, coins flipped. It could have been Ike and Barbara Turner, but Tina won out. It worked. To those who feel it was cavalier treatment and suggest Tina should have at least been consulted during these chauvinistic manoeuvres, Jimmy Thomas gives short shrift. 'When the break-up came years later, Ike said he had the name copyrighted. It was pretty nasty. She was his Dream Child. Nevertheless he can't sing for her. She is her own talent, an individual and a unique visual artist. But without his input she wouldn't have had a hope in hell. There were a load of chicks around who could sing a lot better than Tina. She's a singer of sorts, but she's more of an actress. Women never liked her voice very much. We kept up our popularity on gigs, but the women didn't care too much about Tina's voice. The men liked her because every time they heard her sing, they could visualize what she looked like on stage, in her mini-skirts.'

While the rest of the world saw an apparently perfect rock'n'roll marriage, which they continued to believe in right up until the end of the Seventies, long after the pair had split up, those closest to them, working in the band could see from the outset there was trouble. The 'trouble' turned physical, and in a manner not normally associated with reasonable, sophisticated people.

From the outside it seemed as though Ike did everything possible for Tina, with expense no object. Says Jimmy: 'Tina used to buy these ridiculously expensive clothes to wear on stage, which I thought was a waste. She'd buy a dress from a big store in Dallas for a thousand dollars which wouldn't last that long. She'd sweat it

Ike Turner, mastermind
(*Barry Plummer*)

out on stage. We'd do two shows. The first set would last an hour and we'd come off dripping in sweat. But she looked great. You'd never see anybody else in those kind of clothes.

'She was a star and she always had a sexy act. But Tina was amazingly innocent. She was nothing like the woman she portrayed, the worldly woman who knew it all. She was totally the opposite. After a gig she wouldn't hang out. She'd just go to the hotel and have a meal, watch some TV and go to bed and sleep. The rest of us would be out having a good time!'

After a year on the road, Ike and Tina got married. Did Ike keep Tina under wraps? 'Phew! She was the bread and butter, ha, ha, ha! That's like asking Prince Philip, do you keep the Queen under wraps? Hey, how could you not? Even though Ike was the brain and the show was his thing, Tina Turner was the star. It was a debatable thing, though. Although Tina was a star in her own right, so was Ike in his own way.

'Ike was too shy to push himself, but the way the band worked, and the support they gave Tina on stage . . . that was all Ike keeping it together. It looked like a perfect combination. The problem was their relationship could get pretty stormy.'

Jimmy Thomas found himself caught up in a conflict of loyalties. He was fond of Tina and admired Ike. As a young man he could easily understand Ike's attitudes.

'Ike was a hot-tempered kind of person, an authoritarian. Democratic bands don't do very well. They start floundering and get lost, 'cos you can't have everybody making a decision. You need one ego, one man who is the boss. Then things move and happen. Right from the start it was stormy, but it was good. The downer was, he used to beat the shit out of her. Now the whole world knows about it, and it was never nice. People who make history usually are more intense in their relationships. They burned themselves out on each other. I wasn't surprised when they broke up. I was suprised they lasted so long. I stuck with them the longest, but I left eventually.

'Way before then people started telling Tina how good she really was. She never really paid any attention to stuff like that before.'

As the Revue came to the attention of big bookers, promoters and record companies, they began to whisper in Tina's ear: 'Why don't you try and make it without Ike?'

Says Jimmy: 'A lot of people made her all sorts of promises like – if she ran off from Ike they would make her a big star. But she never had that kind of ego. She was loyal. It was a team. She

Ike strums up a storm while Tina wails

would never dream of doing anything without Ike. Only later she came to realize she could go it alone. How many black eyes did she need? She was getting older and wasn't the same little girl any more.'

Thomas states that the violence started right from the beginning of the marriage, and offers some explanations for the causes.

'It happened from the very outset. Oh yeah. There were so many reasons why he treated her so bad. He had a short fuse. Only the two of them really know what annoyed the other the most. There were never arguments about the music. It was little things. Musically we could all choose our own songs to sing, although the only one who sang original stuff on stage was Tina. The rest of us sang what was happening on the charts. So there were no arguments. If Ike said it was okay, it was okay. Most of their heavy disputes were about other women.

'Ike had two children by his other wife, and Tina had one by him and one by the guy she was fooling around with in the band. Ike and Tina got married when the band became nationally known. For the first couple of years they were messing around. They weren't really lovers. She just hero-worshipped him and looked at him all goo-goo-eyed. Once they got on the road nature took its course, and they got into it. And so between the two of them they had the four boys; Ike Junior who lives in St Louis, Ronnie, who is Ike and Tina's son, Craig who is Tina's son by her former boyfriend and Ike's other son, Mike.'

It was a curious paradox that while Ike was resorting to violence and Tina became the repressed victim of it, the pair could joke and even sing about it, as on the diatribe *Dear John*. Many wondered whether the song was a sort of premonition, or a commentary on an existing state of affairs.

Says Jimmy Thomas: 'Ike wrote it and Tina sang it. Ike took their life and turned it into a song, all about her black eyes and beatings. He was the instigator of all the shit, but she never done anything. She never did nothing wrong. He was the one chasing chicks, and beating up, then he'd sit down and write songs about it and say you gotta sing 'em.

'She'd sing something like "Oh you bastard, but I love you." And it would be true because she worshipped the guy. That's why she took it so long. No other woman would. It was really a perfect acting vehicle for her on stage. You had to see her do it in some boogie joint, not in England at a concert, where it is more clinical. Certain words get lost in transit, which was something she learnt as she became an international star and left America. The expected response to certain key words in some songs wouldn't happen. It wouldn't mean a damn thing to English audiences. It would go right over their heads, while some words would get a laugh she didn't expect, like "shag" – which means a dance in America and something else in England!'

In the race for fame and success, there was little time to stop and think about what was happening to them. 'What was our motivation? It was to enjoy life and get better and better,' says Jimmy.

'As far as Tina was concerned, the main motivation was Ike and her love for him. Behind every step was her desire to please Ike. Now Ike's motivation was . . . for money. And to please Ike! That was the bottom line.'

Tina had no shortage of friends, and while her father had disappeared, her sister still travelled with her on the road to lend moral support. Occasionally, when there had been a bust-up with Ike she would run off and hide with her family. 'She had a hideout,' says Jimmy. 'Eventually he found her and there was one helluva scene. She once ran off in the middle of a tour. Next morning it was "F*** man, anybody seen Tina? The bitch has run off again!"'

There would follow a certain amount of impatient detective work, with hotel porters being harangued and interrogated. If they had been bribed by Tina to keep their mouths shut, then Ike would bribe them to open them again.

'She'd get caught two miles up the road on a bus. He'd drag her off and beat the shit out of her again. That happened several times. It all happened because of frustration. We all felt very sorry for Tina. Not one woman would have traded places with her.'

It seemed none of the band was prepared to help her escape or provide any protection. 'You couldn't, man. If you did it would just result in her getting beat worse. Unless you locked the guy up, how could you take it away from him? All you could do was voice your distaste and displeasure and say you thought it was wrong. You couldn't get involved physically. And anyway nobody had forced her into it and if she really wanted to get away, she could. I felt very sorry for her in that situation, but I also felt, looking at it rationally, that with her runaway attempts, she didn't have to leave certain clues behind. If you want to get away you can plan it. Why in the middle of a tour? The whole world is going to be looking for you. Did she leave clues? That's the only way he found her. 'Cos he isn't that bright. Ha, ha!

'I wasn't alone in thinking that way. We'd say, "Poor old Tina, singing in shades on stage to cover her black eye." Some nights the show would finish, the lights go down and he'd almost drag her off the stage. "Bang, crash, wallop." Everybody knew. But there was nothing you could do about it. And she'd never call the cops. It would be the last thing she'd do. She could be bleeding to death. A strange relationship. Any little thing would upset Ike. It could be her wearing the wrong dress, or her attitude to one of the other girls in the group.'

It wasn't an entirely one-sided battle. Says Jimmy: 'If you are around a person with a short fuse you can pretty much tell what is gonna trigger them off. So you tend to tread lightly. It's like boxing. You dance around. Just ease off man, and disappear until the mood changes. She knew what upset Ike. She was partly to blame and she must see that now that she is beginning to enjoy her life.

'She knew that was just him – the way he was. And I'm pretty sure she ain't sorry she went through it. She's rich, successful and maybe never would have been, if she hadn't gone through that stuff. She can handle a role as a serious actress now because of her life. She's gone through a lot of heavy stuff, and come out of it a successful woman. It's made her a well-rounded human being. It's the irony of being cruel to be kind.'

Meanwhile the show went on, in a series of endless one-night stands, which became such a blur Tina had difficulty remembering where they were. 'Tina is so innocent, she still can't remember if she's in Germany or Switzerland,' says Jimmy. 'In the old days, we'd load up the gear, she'd get in the back seat of the car and be out like a light until we got to the next place, hundreds of miles away. She'd get on stage, do a powerful gig, get back in the car, and be off again. I'd be driving and then singing, sometimes three or four days in a row without any proper sleep.'

Tina had no time for other interests or meeting anybody else outside of the music business. She didn't really have much choice in the matter. 'The only thing we ever considered was music,' says Jimmy. 'Other people in other walks of life and professions just didn't interest us. In fact Tina had no other ambition, except acting. That's what made her so good on stage, and made her image so convincing that she really *was* this raunchy chick. She really was a good actress.

'And that's what she's gonna become. She can still get up there and sweat, but how long can you continue to get up there and growl and snarl and prance? Eventually she must get a bit bored with it all.'

Offering two fingers to the moral majority (*M. Harrison-Goudie*)

OVERLEAF: The Ike & Tina Show socks it to the studio and millions of viewers, as they perform 'live' on Ready, Steady, Go! (*S.K.R. Photos*)

Tina and Jimmy used to act out various skits and sketches on stage to liven up the revue. Sometimes a microphone would go wrong, and they would keep it in the act, and build a skit around it. 'We had a medley with me, Tina and Ike on stage, and a little comedy thing acted out between us.'

Jimmy sang a Dinah Washington, Brook Benton song *If You Wanna Give Me Good Kisses . . . There's A Rockin' Good Way*, with Tina joining him at the mike. The band played softly in the background, and Jimmy asked Tina for a kiss. Ike had his back turned to them, playing his guitar, apparently not knowing what was going down.

Says Jimmy: 'I'd be making up to Tina and it was so real, people started shouting out "Hey Ike!" Ike would turn around in surprise and get into this argument with me, saying, "Look man, this is MY old lady, you're just a singer in the band. Hands off! This ain't even your song." It was so convincing people ran on stage to separate us. Tina was fantastic in her part. She projected so well. But we used to have girls in the group who could wipe the floor with Tina if you were talking about toe for toe singing, range and voice quality-wise.

'Some critics could be pretty cruel and say her voice reminded them of grating metal. But nobody could fault her projection and performance. She put her heart and soul into it. You could see it on her face as she reached for them notes. She was a star! Judy Garland didn't have a great voice, but she had magic. Tina's got that magic too. I never was mad on Tina's singing. She's better now as a singer, because she's got more space to try different kinds of songs. She's much more versatile. You can relax with the Tina Turner of today. But the early Tina was too harsh for you to relax with.'

The harshness, the frantic pace was all typical of the times. America was in a state of turmoil and Ike and Tina's music rocked and wailed against a background of civil rights campaigning and a heightening of racial tension. The musicians and entertainers, whatever their private thoughts about their rights as citizens, wanted to cool out the conflict. They travelled, and 'mixed' and kept a broader, more liberal view. They were ambassadors and says Jimmy: 'We were instrumental in keeping the situation cool. We were brave enough to go out during the marches and protests, when other bands like ours would only play black universities. In fact the band was often a target for activists but we always kept away from them. We'd fight for what we knew, in our own way.'

Ike and Tina had to cope with a dangerous mixture of violence

and prejudice. Sometimes they played gigs where fists and bottles went flying. They dared not stop playing. That would only make things worse.

But they noticed a difference between white and black crowds when a fight broke out. The blacks tended to use knives and guns. 'But the whites would be pretty clean, using fists, and that was it,' recalls Jimmy. 'Our band pioneered the cross-over of black and white audiences. In redneck territory where the people were really prejudiced against black people, once they saw we were in a band, it was cool. Let 'em pass. And they liked the music. There were a lot of bands touring the South and we helped cool out a hot situation.'

There were times when Ike's way of cooling out was to produce a handgun and scare off any would-be assailants. Once Jimmy Thomas was driving a brand new Cadillac fitted out with telephones. He was transporting Ike and Tina, their new white Ikette, Bonnie, and two other black passengers. As they approached a small town along the freeway, a hotrod car loaded with white ruffians drew alongside. They glowered at the white girl in such company and made threatening gestures. Accelerating ahead, they skidded across the road in an attempt to block off the Cadillac. Jimmy escaped down a ramp then came back onto the freeway to block off the hotrod. With the huge Cadillac astride the road, passengers from both vehicles began piling out. Then Ike produced his gun. The rednecks scrambled back into the hotrod and amidst squealing tyres and clouds of smoke from burning rubber, they reversed down the road.

In the South in the late Fifties many of the old segregation laws still applied. Apart from being insulting and ridiculous, they were an irritating anachronism. After one particular night, entertaining white customers, Ike and Tina were in no mood to observe the 'whites only' entrance signs at a roadside eatery.

Jimmy had been driving his charges all night, having topped himself up with 'No Doze' tablets. They arrived in a small town in Mississippi at 5 am. A warning light had come on on the dashboard, and Jimmy wanted to check a slipping fan belt. Ike woke up: 'Where the hell are we? Tina, let's go get something to eat, while Jimmy checks out the car.'

The couple disappeared in the direction of the all-night restaurant adjacent to the garage. Within minutes there was uproar at the counter and the sound of Tina yelling. They were weary travellers, strangers in town, and they hadn't bothered to read the signs. They had gone into the white section and had been refused

Cowgirl in the band. A touch of C&W about Tina's late sixties garb

service. Tina's temper was even more fiery than Ike's in such circumstances.

With a pack of angry rednecks snarling at their heels, Ike and Tina came running back to the car. 'Okay, let's go!' shouted Ike to Jimmy. Their driver obediently hit the starter. It was a brand new, powerful car, but nothing happened. The battery was flat. To their surprise, one of the men from the restaurant came across, and gave the car a shove to get it started.

'There was always a lot of trouble if you were black and driving a Cadillac,' observes Jimmy. Later that night he pulled in to fill up with gas. The attendant was surly and after checking the oil, slammed down the hood. There was more shouting from the passengers, and the white gas station manager came over to apologize: 'There's one thing about America. The customer is always right, black or white!'

*River
Deep
Mountain
High*

River Deep Mountain High

B<small>Y</small> 1965 Ike and Tina Turner has moved to live on the West Coast. They had been through ten record companies in as many years, and there was no shortage of money.

Recalls Jimmy Thomas: 'They had a beautiful house in LA in the Baldwin Hills, at 4263 Olympia Drive. They sold that house after the kids got bigger and bought a larger place, further down the street. They lived out of suitcases a lot of the time, but Tina and Ike had more good times together than bad. They used to have fun together, and laugh, and I think she did the right thing by staying with Ike then. She did it, because she was, in her own way, happy. Tina ain't a party type of person. She's very homely and

likes her garden. And when they weren't on the road, she was at home raising the kids.'

Ike was taking her home-making role too much for granted and began treating her perhaps more like a slave than a wife. Then it seemed there might be a chance for her to break free. One of America's most celebrated record producers, Phil Spector walked into their lives, with far-reaching consequences.

Spector was hailed as a genius. He had created the concept of the all-powerful record producer, invented his own 'Wall of Sound' and instigated some of the most memorable hits of the decade. He was greatly admired by the Beatles and the Rolling Stones and for a brief period was the King Midas of rock music.

One of Spector's greatest artistic achievements was the single *River Deep Mountain High*, performed by Ike and Tina Turner. It was also his most spectacular commercial failure, at least in America. A hit in England, it helped the duo make their first real impact outside the States.

Rare shot of Phil Spector with Ike & Tina, London 1967

Spector was born in the Bronx, New York, in 1940. Later his family moved to Hollywood. As he grew up, Phil became interested in music and dabbled with various instruments. He began writing songs at school. His first big hit was *To Know Him Is To Love Him*, recorded by his own high school group the Teddy Bears, featuring singer Annie Kleinbard. It was a number one smash in both Britain and America. The title and inspiration for the song had come from an inscription on Spector's father's gravestone.

A millionaire at the age of twenty-one, Spector was running his own Philles label which produced a stream of hits, the most notable being *Be My Baby* by the Ronettes, *Da Doo Ron Ron* by the Crystals and *You've Lost That Lovin' Feeling* by the Righteous Brothers. On many of his records he made extensive use of banks of strings, overdubbing and echo to create a Wagnerian, symphonic effect, which he named 'the Wall of Sound', later criticized as the 'Wall of Schlock' by the acerbic New York critic and author Albert Goldman.

As a successful go-getter, he made a lot of enemies, and this was one factor which may have led to the boycotting in America of the astonishing *River Deep Mountain High*, one of the most imaginative and dramatic pop singles of all time.

Spector first spotted Ike and Tina Turner's act when the band were playing at Cyrano's, a Hollywood club on Sunset Strip. The Revue had been out on the road, working hard for eleven months of the year, and they were slick, polished and powerful. Spector was impressed. Above all, he was blown away by Tina's voice. Like Leiber and Stoller, who had created the Coasters to sing their songs, Spector was adept at taking soulful black artists and giving them the best material to work on, backed with the latest studio techniques. Phil approached Ike Turner and asked if he could work with them. His first offer was to include them in a pop music film called *The Big T.N.T. Show*. Another act had dropped out through sickness, would Ike and Tina fill the spot?

It seemed a great idea as far as Ike was concerned, but Phil's real interest was in Tina. He wanted to record her, just as he had several other black singers. More discussions took place, with Tina left in the background. Phil explained to Ike that he would like to produce Tina – alone. At the time he had lost the Righteous Brothers and some of his other acts, like the Ronettes, weren't doing so well. He needed something new. He thought Tina fantastic, although he didn't think much of the production on her previous records.

Bud Dain, of Liberty Records, said that Spector was in effect offering Ike 'an absolute guarantee of hits forever' according to Richard Williams in his book *Out Of His Head* (Abacus), about the life of Spector.

Spector offered Ike Turner twenty thousand dollars for the right to produce Tina as a solo artist. Ike had just changed labels from Loma, the Warner Bros offshoot, to Kent, and as usual, wasn't happy with the results – or lack of them. Ike took the twenty thousand dollars, but it was on the condition that he himself had nothing to do with the sessions and stayed out of the studio while Spector was at work with Tina. Ike graciously agreed.

Phil invited Tina over to his house to show her a new song he had written, with her in mind, with Jeff Barry and Ellie Greenwich. It was *River Deep Mountain High*. During the writing session they came up with four other songs including *I Can Hear Music*. But it was *River Deep* which thrilled Tina, who said later: 'For the first time in my life, it wasn't R&B. I finally had a chance to sing.'

Said Spector: 'The whole thing about *River Deep* was the way I could feel that strong bass line. That's how it started. And then Jeff came up with the opening line. I wanted a tender song about a chick who loved somebody very much . . . so we came up with a rag doll, and "I'm going to cuddle you like a little puppy."'

The song was carefully constructed to suit Tina's range, including her ability to hit deep notes, just as Spector had produced *You've Lost That Lovin' Feeling* for the Righteous Brothers.

River Deep was recorded at Gold Star studios with Spector controlling every note. The song had taken two weeks to write, but many more man hours were put into the production. Jack Nitzsche did the arrangements, and there were masses of overdubs, and endless mixing and re-recording. The singing was straightforward, except for the opening line 'When I was a little girl,' which had an odd metre. Tina had to sing it over and over again, drenched in sweat and clad only in her bra and pants, trying to get it right. Spector was coaxing the best out of her, and was determined to get it perfect. In the end, the cost of the single rocketed to over twenty-two thousand dollars, which was more money than was spent on the average album, ten years later.

The session had begun on the night of 7 March 1966 and the final product was released on the A-side of Philles 131. In England it was released on London HLU 10046 coupled with *I'll Keep You Happy* in May 1966. It caused a sensation in Britain where it was a

Ike & Tina on top British sixties TV show Ready, Steady, Go! (*Peter Stuart*)

82

huge hit. But in the States it was a failure. Said Spector: 'People just didn't care for it, the disc jockeys wouldn't play it. It reached the point of antagonism, where people said, "Who does he think he is? He never takes us to dinner." Resentment built up. I thought the record was good. I really liked it, anyway.'

Ike Turner, who had nothing to do with the song, even though his name appeared on the credits, was equally disappointed. He laid the blame on racism in the American music scene, which wouldn't accept a white-style pop song from a black artist.

Said Ike: 'If you had not put Tina's name on there but put "Joe Blow", then the Top 40 stations would have accepted it for being a pop record. But they had branded Tina Turner as being an R&B artist. I think the main reason that *River Deep* didn't make it in America was that the R&B stations wouldn't play it because they thought it was pop, and the pop stations wouldn't play it because they thought it was R&B. And it didn't get played at all.' Ike cited *River Deep* as one of his (all-time) favourite records along with, surprisingly enough, *Good Vibrations* by the Beach Boys.

Jeff Barry thought that part of the problem was the 'mix' – which meant the lead vocal was buried in the track. He thought Phil had overcooked the production with too many strings, too many musicians. And Spector had made some comments about the standards of commercial radio which upset the nation's disc jockeys. Others suggested that Spector had been blacklisted for not paying payola, the outlawed system of bribing DJs for plays.

Quite the opposite happened in Britain, where Decca promotions man Tony Hall wrote to radio DJs personally and asked them to play the record on its merits. He was also helped by the new pirate radio stations operating from ships moored around the coast. The pirates began playing the record, hotly followed by the BBC who were trying to win back lost audiences with more pop music.

The record got to number two in the UK singles charts. But Spector was so embittered and embarrassed by its failure in America he went into seclusion and did not produce another record for three years.

Tina was very proud of the record. During the *River Deep* sessions she also cut the B-side, *I'll Keep You Happy*, and the follow-up A-side, later released in England, a new version of Martha and the Vandellas' song *A Love Like Yours (Don't Come Knocking Every Day)* composed by Eddie and Brian Holland and Lamont Dozier. It was released on London (HLU 10083), in October 1966 and the B-side was a Jeff Barry, Ellie Greenwich song *Hold On Baby* which sounded similar to *River Deep*, and was equally fast and noisy.

A year later came the third Spector-produced Ike and Tina Turner single *I'll Never Need More Than This* (London HLU 10155), coupled with *Save The Last Dance For Me* and released in September 1967. There were two more cuts featuring Tina, called *A Man Is A Man Is A Man* and *Two To Tango* which were scheduled as American singles, but weren't released. In 1966 London (the Decca-owned label) released a *River Deep Mountain High* album. Apart from the Spector productions it also featured reworkings of old songs, produced by Ike, including *It's Gonna Work out Fine*, *I Idolise You* and *A Fool In Love*.

Phil Spector got out of the record business at the end of 1966 thoroughly disheartened and disillusioned and only came back when he was re-introduced to John Lennon by Allen Klein, which led to his re-mixing the Beatles' *Get Back* album and producing many of John Lennon's post-Beatles records.

Jimmy Thomas watched the outcome of *River Deep* with great excitement, because the Rolling Stones had pronounced the record one of the wonders of the age and invited the entire Ike and Tina Revue to come to England and tour with them.

'*River Deep* was gonna be the big deal. That was gonna be everything. That brought us our first trip to England. It was number two in the charts there, but it wasn't a hit in the States because Phil Spector was really another Ike figure. The industry didn't like Phil during that period. He had a beef with them, and his name was mud. When the record was a hit in England it was like two fingers in the air from Phil to the American music scene.

'The size of Phil and Ike's egos were so huge that if they had tried to work together in the studio it would have been like putting two dinosaurs in a cage together. No way could they work together. Ike wouldn't even go into the studio when Tina was being produced by Phil and Phil wouldn't have him there! It would have led to fisticuffs because they're both crazy. Both nuts! Phil was highly attracted to Tina's voice and as Spector was such a powerful man, Ike suspected Tina would be tempted to go fulltime with Phil.'

Apart from the British hit, there were other rewards for Ike. He was offered a job as A&R man for the Philles label. But this resulted in only one single being produced, for the Ikettes. Later Ike would continue his cruising around the various record companies of America, and he signed to Pompeii Records for two years. Ike and Tina made three albums for them including *So Fine*,

Black Man's Soul and *Cussin', Cryin' And Carryin' On*.

Next he signed to Blue Thumb in 1968 and made two albums for them, *Outta Season*, and *The Hunter*. The former was released in Britain on Liberty (LBS 83241), in June 1969, and the latter on EMI's progressive rock label, Harvest (SHSP 4001) in September 1970. The title track *The Hunter* was a hit in the States.

In 1969 the duo had signed with Minit, which was taken over by Liberty, which in turn became part of United Artists. This provided a stable home for Ike and Tina until the final break-up of the partnership in 1975.

The Blue Thumb period was set in motion by one of Ike's old friends, Bob Krasnow, who had become president of the label. Krasnow produced several hits for Ike and Tina including *The Hunter* and also a version of Otis Redding's hit *I've Been Loving You Too Long*. The latter song became a vehicle for overt sexuality on stage, with Tina virtually making love to the microphone, a phallic symbol in her caressing hands and lips.

The song became a central part of the Revue, as Tina traded innuendos with Ike, while the Ikettes in their mini-skirts and flailing wigs, flung themselves into the dance of the two veils. Although the Sixties had a reputation for 'swinging' and being the dawn of the age of liberation, rock music was still largely an earnest activity. Public venues were strictly controlled by an old guard of management who pounced on anything that might be construed as obscene. When P. J. Proby, the young Texan singer, came to England and enjoyed massive popularity after a hit with *Somewhere*, his career was virtually ruined by bans imposed on him, after he tore his trouser legs a few times on stage. The trousers were carefully stitched so they would tear more easily, and all that was revealed were somewhat knobbly knees. Yet the authorities threw up their hands in horror.

Against this background, it was to be expected that Tina might run into some flak. And yet somehow she not only escaped censure in Europe, but her erotic routines were welcomed and lauded as art, which indeed they were. Tina's act undoubtedly fell under the heading of 'cabaret' and so all was forgiven. And those theatre managers who found Proby's tattered breeches so offensive, queued for a glimpse of stocking in the orchestra pit.

The tights revolution had taken its grip on the female population, much to the chagrin of males who missed stocking tops and all the elaborate engineering of old-style suspenders and garters. Tina and the Ikettes' blatant disregard for new underwear styles, caused a frisson of excitement that extended to the press.

A glimpse of stocking is still pleasantly shocking (*Andre Csillag*)

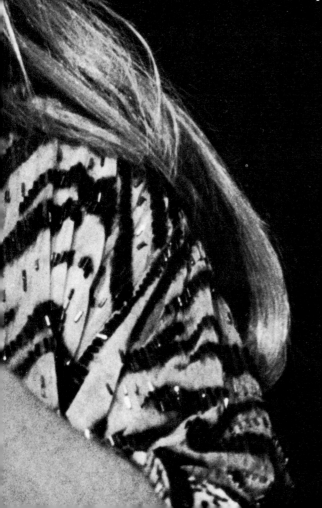

'I've been loving you too long' (*S. Fowler/LFI*)

Wrote Alan Lewis in the *Melody Maker* after seeing one of their shows in Paris: 'Ike and Tina Turner are the most exciting stage act I have ever seen. And if that sounds like an absurdly breathless and subjective thing to say, then you'll have to forgive me. It's quite impossible to be subjective after you've experienced Tina Turner singing *I've Been Loving You Too Long.*'

Alan, describing it as 'the climax of their act', added: 'It is quite literally an apocalyptic experience. Emotionally, sensually, spiritually and, if you must, artistically, it is the most shattering performance in rock.'

During the course of the song, Tina sang the Redding lyrics in husky, breathless fashion while Ike fed her gospel-tinged blues guitar licks. Then the tempo increased and the mood intensified, until the stage lights were cut, leaving Tina alone in the spotlight. 'Her face contorted with anguish and ecstasy, she moaned and screamed out responses to Ike's insistent, unseen wailing,' reported Lewis.

Tina caressed the microphone while singing 'Baby, you can

make me do anything you want me to do . . . buy you anything you want me to buy . . . oh baby, sock it to me . . . oh, oh, oh.' In answer to those who might shout from the gallery, 'Throw a bucket of water over them!' the critic claimed that it was musical and erotic triumph. 'It leaves you wondering why the hell they've had to wait so long to get the recognition they deserve.'

The routine earned Tina yet another title, as the 'Queen Of Raunch'n'Roll'. The *New York Times* called her show 'pornographic'. Tina always tried to play down this aspect of her work in interviews however, pointing out that the so-called pornographic content only applied to the one number.

'It's the only way to sing *I've Been Loving You Too Long*. It's a sort of sex thing, between Ike and myself. I do little things to the microphone. It fits in today, but you couldn't have done it yesterday very easily. It is a little embarrassing,' she conceded, 'to a point. It's the thing to do today. Well, it's embarrassing to the women, but it's like acting. I'm sure a lot of actors don't feel very comfortable with some of their parts, and I guess I'm an actress. I wouldn't take it out of our show because I think it's a part that people come to see.'

Some critics felt that the song had been solely responsible for helping Ike and Tina rise above the soul circuit and out into the major venues, auditoriums and sports stadiums of America. The number had been devised by Ike to exploit Tina's sexuality, a fact which did not escape writers, or representatives of the newly-burgeoning women's liberation movements. Tina's act, with Ike as the macho mastermind and she as the slave girl, flew in the face of contemporary thinking. The result was to make their act a smash hit and prove that once again, Ike was right.

Tina quite cheerfully admitted that Ike was acting out his male dominance, while she was symbolizing her devotion. If it was only an act, then it seemed to work to both their advantage. Said Tina: 'Ike has the last word. That says it all. He's the organizer of the show, and nothing goes through until it is okayed by Ike. If it was up to me to settle down and stop singing, I'm sure I would. But Ike is reaching out for an expression of man and woman. It is his goal, and I think every woman does this sort of thing for her man.'

While most men would count themselves lucky if they had a cup of tea in bed and a pair of clean socks ready for the day, Ike obviously expected a sexual pageant, twice-nightly. And an integral part of the show was the ever popular Ikettes. Explained Tina: 'As far as choreographing the show I get together with the girls and we work on it. But then we take our ideas to Ike because he's the organizer. We have certain rules for the girls. They're women, but if they like their jobs they'll do what they're told. I tell them to keep it clean!'

Tina spelt out the Ikettes' house rules: 'The main rule is no bumps or grinds. We do a lot of moving, but it's all from the hips. There is no one too valuable for this show that we can't get rid of them. They have to be good dancers. They have to be able to move and pick up quickly on everything.

'If I get a girl who can't catch on to things quickly, I usually don't keep her. Because we do a lot of changing, and creating, right on the stage. We don't take a lot of time out to rehearse. We just do whatever comes into our heads.'

Tina reiterated the need for long hair in the act. 'I like long hair. It adds to the action. Some of the girls have worn short hair, the natural look, but they usually switch back to long hair because it accentuates the movement. You know, hair is one of the best things a woman has going for her beauty.'

Tina was always amused by the reaction her performance caused and the image it conveyed. 'I've always been shocked to see how big I seem on film or TV, even in photographs,' she told Stann Findelle in the *New Musical Express*. 'People always think I am some kind of damn Amazon woman. We always do everything nice . . . and rough! We don't wear no jewellery or nothing else on stage that could break off. Our dancing is half-stage and half-street. In spite of what everyone says we try to keep it as clean as possible. Notice, I always shoot the hips to the side, not to the front. We don't do no dry screwin' up there. No cheap shots.'

The band gathered momentum and new generations of fans came along, curious about the origins of their act.

'When I first met Ike in St Louis he had always used two male singers. I thought we could get it on better with three females. I had always danced, so that would make it four. Then the "Shindig" show and white Go Go dancing came along and gave us some more fuel. I wanted to break out of the limited plasticity of so many soul acts, with the three guys mincing their steps, like jive choreography. I like the girls to be pretty. We can't use any uglies,' she claimed, contradicting the Jimmy Thomas philosophy. 'But it's a certain kind of raw pretty,' she conceded. 'Good figure, long legs, shapely. But if she's tall, thin, ugly and a great singer, fo'get it! Oh, I've fixed up some gals who were almost ugly but had great bodies. I've got a whole grooming programme I put new recruits through that can fix 'em up with the hair and all.

'Actually I don't want 'em too pretty-pretty. Then they wanna

go out and be solo artists. Bonnie Bramlett (one of their few white girl singers), was a fine singer, looked real fine. But she just took off after a couple of nights.' Tina revealed they had also run into trouble in the South for having a 'mixed' line-up. 'There was integration grumblings about it down South and lady cops were always gettin' ready to bust us for being obscene anyhow, so there was no use giving them something else to grumble about. She was an exception, but for the most part I find white girls are too frail and fragile to take what I put 'em through. They are always coming down with sniffles or bronchitis or fractures or somethin'.'

At one time Tina thought of having a reunion show featuring all her various Ikettes but then gave it up as a bad idea. 'Maybe it wouldn't have been so hot,' she told Findelle. 'I notice once they get away from me, they go to fat and out of shape. They dance like Brontosaurs. They go from Ikettes to Ickettes! When a girl comes in, they usually put on that cute, cuddly façade, the way women are supposed to be, with their legs closed together in public. The whole attitude. I say to them: "Come on honey, spread 'em apart. You ain't putting nothing over on me. You're gonna have to spread 'em on stage. Even with those snoopy photographers shootin' up on ya." You can't be embarrassed easily and be an Ikette.

'You know, I don't think we ever set out to be sexy,' said Tina. 'But I could never just stand still and sing. I have to move and sometimes audiences can be a little cold and they need humouring.'

Years later she looked back on the days when Ike pushed her into increasing vulgarity on stage with *I've Been Lovin' You Too Long* with some distaste. 'Oh that song became a nightmare. It's like you're feeling real good at an office party and you take off your clothes and streak, but you don't want to run around like that every day, right? Well since the audiences loved that number, Ike decided we should always do it, and I was trapped. Ike was totally dominating. Everything was done when he wanted and how he wanted. I had no say. I was just yes-ing. Once I got on stage that was my outlet, that was my freedom, just to sing it all out. But when I left the stage, the lights went out.'

The use of wigs by both Tina and the Ikettes goes back many years, and Jimmy Thomas explains why the tradition has lasted. 'In the old pre-Beatles days black people used to mimic white people with their hair. It was okay, routine enough. They thought the only way to be accepted was to look the Hollywood way. It was understandable and completely valid. Then after the Beatles

Ikettes not 'Ickettes'

OVERLEAF: Ike's Domain: Flashing thighs as the Ikettes kick ass, at the Hammersmith Odeon, London, 1972 (*Robert Ellis*)

everybody got loose and started to look at themselves. There was Martin Luther King's leadership, the Freedom Riders, integration in the schools and black people decided, "Okay, we're cool. Let's just be us." Everybody came out of their wigs! Well most of them did, except Tina. She never did come out of her wig, and I think it was mostly Ike's fault. You can't blame Ike for it now, but in them days it was. We'd be travelling in the car between towns and she'd take the wig off, and he wouldn't be too happy about it, especially the closer we got to town. I don't know why he didn't like her hair, because there was nothing wrong with it!

'Now we are seeing the last dying embers of Ike's influence on Tina's performances in her present-day stage act. I'm glad she has changed her act a bit now and put an end to the Ikettes hangover. She's got rid of the girls, and I'm hoping the next step will be to take off the wig. I love the wig, but it's been a long time! Ha, ha, ha! She's worn wigs for as far back as I can remember. You folks ain't seen her without it, I promise you. And don't ask me why. I could understand it in the early days when the accent was on action and the long hair accentuated it. But she's got her own nice hair. At one time people didn't talk about it, and most people didn't know. But Jim Davidson sent her up on his TV show singing *I Can't Stand The Rain* – and his wig fell off. Then everybody in England cottoned on. It's only recently that she has been mimicked, because she got so famous, but before that people never used to talk about it.'

The showbusiness traditions that Tina holds dear were firmly rooted in those tough times when they were working night after night, touring around America, waiting for the big break and a record company that would want to hold onto them for longer than a few months. Ike and Tina were 'paying their dues' but they had a lot of fun in the process.

'Tina's stamina was just natural,' recalls Jimmy Thomas. 'The sets were long and it was hard work, especially the way she sang. It was peak energy all the time. In those early days we could only hear black music on the black radio stations. The only time we heard black music on white stations was when they had a special programme set aside. In Memphis they had a station which featured a programme called "In the Groove", three times a week. They played twenty minutes of black music. That's all the public could get, the only way white audiences might hear Ike and Tina Turner.

'Then the black stations began to spring up and the music got more publicized. Elvis helped a lot. If Tina had been a bit earlier, she would have gone into a blues band. Willie Mae Thornton used to sing with that rasping style.'

Ike and Tina were about to bid farewell to the chitlin' circuit, thanks to the sudden interest of the new wave of rock performers, but in the meantime there were a few more adventures, a few more highways to burn up.

'Sometimes we'd drive five hundred miles to one gig,' says Jimmy. 'They would get into the back seat and we'd be off. Yes, I did all the driving, and I loved it, and they wouldn't trust anybody else at the wheel. I loved driving Cadillacs, especially late at night. America is such a vast place, you can drive thousands of miles with hardly a stop. Ike and Tina didn't feel comfortable riding with anybody else. They couldn't drive to the next gig themselves, they had to have a driver . . . me! I had to do a show as well, but it was by choice. That's how I discovered America. Ike and Tina would wake up and they'd be there. They became my family. We had a brand new Cadillac every year. It became home along with the hotel room. Everything else was a blur. Tina was so isolated, she didn't know what town she was in half the time.'

The Revue began to play bigger venues as soul music grew and diversified.

'We did the package shows, playing theatres like the Apollo in New York, the Royal in Baltimore, the Uptown in Philadelphia, and the Regal in Chicago. We'd play those then go down the Eastern Seaboard and into Eastern Texas and back up again. We would be on the package tours with Smokey and the Miracles, Jerry Butler and Chuck Jackson. People might think butter wouldn't melt in their mouths but it was all an act, as I discovered. They conducted their lives in a very tough way. Some artists are made that way by society but some are just born that way.

'The paranoia of some of the artists who got ripped off was understandable, but some, like Little Richard, could still be pleasant, accessible and coherent. Others would come across so heavy and bitter, as if they blamed the whole world for their ills, and that wasn't right.

'Ike went off into a heavy cocaine thing which can alter one's personality and lead to over-indulgence. That might have been one of the things which contributed to the break-up. But when I was there, Ike wouldn't even drink. You had to twist the cat's arm to take a sip of alcohol. He would fine cats in the band he found drinking when we were supposed to be gigging. He didn't like it. Everybody thought he was hiked up on something, but he never was. Something happened to change him in the couple of years after I left.'

Honky Tonk Woman

Honky Tonk Woman

*B*RITISH ROCK stars in the Sixties were a breed of pioneers who set trends and became arbiters of taste in fashion, attitudes and music. They had greater power and influence than latterday stars because the vast majority of their followers had considerably less access to the fountain of ideas – America.

In the Eighties, with video, multi-channel TV and the emergence of street fashions and sub-teen culture, the artists find it difficult to keep abreast, let alone ahead of the times. Back in the Sixties teenagers were avid pop fans and had been since the advent of rock'n'roll. They were, however, rationed and restricted by what the local record companies would release and what the BBC radio and TV networks would play.

Fans were familiar with the hits of the established American rock'n'roll stars like Elvis Presley, Bill Haley and Jerry Lee Lewis, and there *were* several black artists who had broken through, like Fats Domino and Little Richard, but the vast number of blues, R&B and soul artists then operating in the States, remained an unknown quantity abroad.

Says Ian 'Stu' Stewart, the keyboard player with the Rolling Stones since their inception, who now runs his own band called Rocket 88: 'In those days we didn't know about records like Ike Turner's *Rocket 88*. They were completely unavailable in Britain. In fact we took our name "Rocket 88" from a Pete Johnson number.'

It was the Rolling Stones who helped most to advance the cause of black American music by espousing it and championing many underrated artists. In fact the whole British beat boom of the early Sixties came from the discovery by enthusiastic young players, of the kind of music that rock'n'roll had been built on. As the Beatles turned on to the Isley Brothers and recorded *Twist And Shout*, so the Stones down south in Richmond, raved about Chuck Berry and Bo Didley. Their records were released and sold well in Britain only after the Stones had popularized tunes like *Come On* and *Around And Around*, while *I'm A Man*, *Road Runner* and *Sweet Little Sixteen* became the staple fare of every aspiring R&B group in the country.

There were many other blues purists and champions who contributed to the increasing awareness of the rich treasure house of music waiting to be unlocked, people like Alexis Korner, Chris Barber, Cyril Davies, Long John Baldry, John Mayall and Eric Burdon. The Stones – in particular Mick Jagger and Keith Richard – were the most consistent and effective catalysts though, through their spontaneous enthusiasm and power over the media.

As students they had delved into the blues and discovered the delights of Jimmy Reed, Willie Dixon and Chuck'n'Bo. Later, on their travels in America with the Stones, they saw at first hand at such venues as the Apollo in New York, artists like James Brown and Ike and Tina Turner.

In 1966 the Stones were at the peak of their first wave of popularity, with *Satisfaction* still causing shock waves and new releases pouring off the presses including *Nineteenth Nervous Breakdown* and *Paint It Black*. When they went out on tour it was a signal for audience hysteria that equalled the frenzy unleashed by the Beatles.

Into this madness the Stones were determined to introduce

PREVIOUS PAGE: The Revue hits London, 1971 (*Barry Wentzell*)

The team . . . hard at work (*Barry Plummer*)

104

artists they liked and admired and wanted to expose to their somewhat unsophisticated fans. *River Deep Mountain High* gave them the excuse to invite to Britain the complete Ike and Tina Turner Revue, including Jimmy Thomas. He has vivid memories of that early tour as both acts barnstormed around the cinema and theatre circuit.

'It was weird man. It was good fun. But it was *so* different. It was the first time we had been out of the boundaries of the United States. We had been used to working really hard on stage. In fact we worked so hard, we danced on our ears. The whole object of the game was to win that audience. Lay it on 'em. When we played our first show in England with the Stones, none of us could believe it.

'We came out popping and kicking and zapping, and we got a nice reaction. Then it was "And now, the Rolling Stones." Just noise. Screams, yells, howls, all the way through the performance. Strange to us.

'The Stones would stand in the wings and watch us and say "Wow . . . nice." And we'd watch them from the wings and think "Wow . . . strange!" They could be playing out of tune, out of key, anything, nobody knew. It was just girls screaming and yelling. We had never seen anything like that. We could hear Mick singing out of tune through the monitors, but it didn't matter. It was fascinating. And we went down well too. Made a lot of friends. It was great. I loved it. Tina got to know Mick real well. And P. P. Arnold. She was one of the Ikettes when we came over, and she had an affair with Mick. He was producing Chris Farlowe, and he used me, Pat Arnold and another Ikette called Rose to do the backing vocals.'

Between tour dates, the Stones and the Turners hung out together, jammed, made records and went to clubs. They thoroughly enjoyed the phenomenon of Swinging London. They were especially impressed when Mick turned up to take them for a ride in his latest car. It was a vehicle that the insular Americans, used to lumbering Cadillacs, had never seen before. It was a brand new Aston Martin, pride of the British sports car industry.

Mick's driving terrified his guests, especially as he appeared to be driving on the 'wrong' side of the road. Says Jimmy: 'Pat Arnold started going out to dinner with Mick driving, and she was officially an Ikette and Ike didn't like that stuff!

'He guarded his girls jealously. But Pat was glimpsing another world. Mick tried to get her to stay and succeeded. He tried to get me to stay as well. Rose was getting married and so she had to go

'A lioness on heat.' Tina in full fury, 1972

107

back home anyway. I wasn't ready to stay then, although it was really swinging in London and the club scene was happening.'

Apart from playing at the major theatres with the Stones, Ike and Tina were booked in to play for a more select clientèle at the London 'in' clubs, with extraordinary results.

'Oh, that was hilarious man,' says Jimmy. 'We were used to the chitlin' circuit, playing sweaty joints. That part was okay. But we were sorta surprised that the clubs were that small in London for a band of our size to play. I'll never forget the Scotch of St James. We played there two or three times on both our British tours.' (They came back again in 1968.)

'It was really small. Our show was full of kicks and dancing, sweat and funk flying everywhere. We were standing face to face with our audiences. Great gigs. And we played a little club off the Cromwell Road, called Blaises, and Hatchetts in Piccadilly as well. We'd see all our mates in the clubs and there was no big deal. We couldn't wait until night fell.

'Mick didn't sit in with us on those trips. He didn't have the nerve! I remember some crazy jam sessions in Detroit, when Marvin Gaye sat in with Ike. But Mick and the Stones were pretty overawed by us. We were overawed by the crowd reaction to the Stones, rather more than by their musicianship.

'We couldn't hear Brian Jones play for a whole tour. All we could really hear was Charlie Watts' bass drum. Then one night in Coventry I heard some stinging blues coming out of a dressing room. It was Brian Jones playing the guitar. He was in there all on his own. And the guy was good. We didn't know anybody could play like that in England.'

One of the highlights of that first visit was when the Ike and Tina Turner Revue appeared on the ATV show *Ready, Steady, Go!* which was aired live on Friday, 30 September, 1966. The drive and excitement of their performance won them many new fans in Britain. They had several singles released that year. As well as *River Deep* there was *Tell Her I'm Not Home, Anything You Wasn't Born With, A Love Like Yours, Goodbye So Long*, and *Somebody (Somewhere) Needs You*.

As a result of all the interest, Pat Arnold stayed on in Britain and recorded for Andrew Oldham's Immediate label and went out with an English backing group the Nice, featuring Keith Emerson, Davey O'List, Lee Jackson, Ian Hague and later Brian Davidson on drums. This band later went out on their own without Pat, and became hailed as pioneers of progressive rock, before splitting up to make way for Emerson's new group, Emerson, Lake and Palmer.

Tina took the 'lioness' tag to heart (*Barry Plummer*)

Pat worked on more sessions for Immediate and then in 1967 had a big hit with her powerful version of the Cat Stevens' song *The First Cut Is The Deepest*. She also released a solo album *Kafunta* produced by Mick Jagger and Steve Marriott.

Ian Stewart, 'the sixth Rolling Stone' remembers the sensation Ike and Tina caused on their tour with the Stones, and feels the group did a lot to help other American acts, often at a financial loss and without much thanks from the artists involved.

'What happened was, that tour in 1966 was the first the Stones had control over. They had done tours with Little Richard for Don Arden (promoter) and odd things for Robert Stigwood, but the tour with Tina was the first time they effectively organized things themselves and had a say in the running. And they did what they have always done ever since, which was to bring to people's attention good artists, rather than any old rubbish. They were very fond of Tina, and thought very highly of Ike as well.

'On stage with us the Revue was still doing covers of other people's stuff, Motown things. I don't actually remember them doing *River Deep* then. It was a full tour, if not a long one, which began in September 1966. They had another guitar player, a white guy, as well as Ike, piano, bass, drums and a couple of trumpets.

They had a piano player with them called Blue. He was an old man but he played really well. He was a friend of Ike's. They all went down very well. Mick got on really well with Tina, and I personally found Ike very friendly. After the shows, I asked him to show me a few things on piano, and he always did.

'But there was an awful atmosphere with the Ikettes and the whole Revue thing. It was a very strange thing about Ike. He had his own secretary and she looked very much like Tina. She was very beautiful, and one of the Ikettes also looked like Tina, and was just as beautiful. I think he was having affairs with both of them, and there were fights with Tina about it. She ended up with black eyes. They had one of those volatile relationships, you might say! I used to keep out of the way, but you could see what was going on. There were terrible shout-ups backstage and sometimes it got physical.

'They were always late arriving at the theatres, and in those days the theatre managers ruled. But when they did get there on time, they would start playing some warm-up music and it would be really great. I think Mick got a lot from watching Tina on stage, and they really hit it off. There was nothing between them, but she was always very helpful and friendly.

'Then the Beatles announced that they weren't going to play live any more, they were going to stay in the studios and spend all their time and lots of money making records. So Mick said, "Right – this is the way from now on. We're going to spend all *our* time in the studios making records." So the Stones made *Their Satanic Majesties Request* and didn't tour from 1966 to 1969. Then there was a lovely lossmaking tour in December 1969. We had Chuck Berry, B. B. King and Ike and Tina on the tour with us.

'I remember at Madison Square Garden Janis Joplin got up. She was going to sing with Ike and Tina, but she didn't last five minutes. She got blown away. She was completely out of it. The Stones put on a lot of artists who had previously appealed to exclusively black audiences. They gave Stevie Wonder, B. B. King, and Chuck Berry exposure to millions of white American and British kids who would never have seen them.

'The Stones were all delighted with Ike and Tina's success and particularly Tina's when she went solo. She was always a real sweetheart. If the Stones gave her career a boost, well she deserved it. We thought she was wonderful.'

The feelings were mutual. At the start of the Seventies, Ike and Tina were earning thirty thousand dollars a week, and they were being given star treatment. 'We owe most of it to the Rolling

112

Stones,' said Tina. 'When they asked us to join them when they toured the States in '69, that was when it all started to happen for us. That was when we started to get through to the rock audiences. And before that they were the ones who brought us over to England in '66 and got us known there. They turned us on to rock.'

The British experience was an eye-opener and morale booster for the Turners. It also encouraged them to widen their musical scope, and as rock bands began writing their own material, rather than rely on the R&B hits of the past, so the Turners began to use rock songs in their act and on record.

Tina recalled how contact with the Rolling Stones first developed, in an interview with *Rolling Stone*'s Ben Fong-Torres: 'Mick was a friend of Phil Spector. And the time we cut *River Deep* Mick was around at Gold Studios in L.A. I remembered him but I never talked to him. He's not the type to make you feel you could just come up and talk to him. Mick thought the record was great, and he caught our act a couple of times. Mick wasn't dancing at the time. He always said he liked to see girls dance. So he was excited about our show, and he thought it would be different for the people of England.

'I remember I wasn't mingling too much. Ike and I were having problems at the time, and we stayed mad at each other. But I'd always seen Mick in the wings. I thought "Wow, he must really be a fan." I'd come out and watch him occasionally. They'd play music and Mick would beat the tambourine. He wasn't dancing.' (Tina's memories of Jagger's stage style during that period were confirmed when old *Ready Steady Go!* shows were repeated on British TV in 1985, some twenty years later.)

'Lo and behold,' said Tina, 'when Mick came to America he was doing everything! So then I knew what he was doing in the wings. He learned a lot of steps and I tried to teach him the Popcorn and other steps we were doing. But he can't do 'em like that. He has to do it his way.'

Back in the States the Turners' act was still categorized as R&B and when they had a hit with *Bold Soul Sister* in L.A. it was only on a black station. The white stations refused to play it or *I've Been Loving You Too Long* until it sold so many copies anyway, it had to be put on the play lists. The pressure was on for Ike and Tina to make more commercial records if they wanted to get wider exposure.

The couple were in a record shop in Seattle when they heard the Beatles' record *Come Together* and Tina said: 'Oh, Ike – I gotta do

113

it on stage! I love that record.' She thought it would be good for the stage act, along with another number, the Stones' *Honky Tonk Woman*. 'That's me!' she exclaimed.

In 1969, when Ike and Tina were invited on to the Stones' American tour, the resultant exposure and the heavy rock numbers they now included in the act made them overnight sensations in their own country – at last. They hit the front pages of the top fashion and news magazines, including *Vogue* and *Playboy*.

Tina roared through John Lennon's lyrics on *Come Together* with her own brand of savage attack and rave reviews came pouring in. A major record company, Liberty, began to take an interest in the act, and although they had been recording for Bob Krasnow's Blue Thumb label, they had no contract with him. Krasnow gave his blessing, and they signed an exclusive contract with the bigger company. The result was the *Outta Season* album followed by *Come Together* (Liberty LBS 83350) released in August 1970. The single *Come Together* coupled with *Honky Tonk Woman* (Liberty LBF 15303) came out in February. They also recorded another rock standard – Creedence Clearwater's *Proud Mary*, which remained in Tina's act for many years.

Said Tina: 'When we cut the album we were lacking a few tunes, so we said, "Well – let's just put in a few things that we're doing on stage." That's how *Proud Mary* came about. I had loved it when it first came out. We auditioned a girl and she had sung *Proud Mary* and Ike said, "You know, I forgot all about that tune." And I said we should do it but change it. So Ike played the guitar and we just sort of jammed into a black version. It wasn't planned. My mother listened to blues on the radio, B. B. King and all that, but rock'n'roll was more me, and when that sort of music came on, I never could sit down. I've always wanted to move.'

Ike, however, suggested that he had to coax Tina into listening to more hard rock. He said to her: 'You are going to have to sing it, so you may as well like it.'

Ike signed to Liberty Records (which became United Artists) in January 1970 and the company guaranteed to pay him $150,000 a year in return for two albums per year. A year later the option came up for renewal. By now Ike had plans for expansion and he wanted to find an escape from endless touring by building his own studio, which would become his dream factory. Ike had delivered only one album, albeit a bestseller, in *Come Together*. He needed another $150,000 and as Liberty trusted his judgement, they gave him the money. Ike got his studio and the company were given the hit single *Proud Mary* coupled with *Funkier Than A Mosquita's*

Tweeter (Liberty LBF 15432) in January 1971. Later that year Ike put in a request for a further $150,000 and he got it – a total of $450,000 in advances. It was not surprising then that Ike and Tina Turner settled down for a long stay with Liberty/UA. The company had to recoup its investment.

After the *Come Together* album came *The Hunter* in September 1970, *Workin' Together* (Liberty LBS 83455) released in February 1971 and *Live In Paris* (Liberty LBS 84368) in the summer of 1971. This was a double live album followed by another similar live set, *What You Hear Is What You Get* (UA UAD 6005/6) in September.

Some critics thought that these live performances were disappointing in comparison to the more raunchy R&B they had played so effectively for so long in the Sixties, but of course they sold much better. It was all part of the modernization process, like re-naming the Kings of Rhythm with the more up-to-date sounding 'Family Vibes'.

The live double set was recorded in Carnegie Hall, New York, and achieved gold status. *Proud Mary* went gold and was given a Grammy award. Together with *The Fantastic Ike and Tina* released on the budget-priced Sunset label in March 1971 it was a productive, busy time. *Life* magazine, *Look*, *Harper's Bazaar*, *Ebony* and *Newsweek* all devoted centre-spread articles to the couple. As they guested on all the major networked TV chat shows, and performed at such venues as the International Hotel, Las Vegas, and in Central Park, New York, it seemed everything they had ever worked for was finally coming their way.

It was too late for Jimmy Thomas. He had quit the Revue and decided to try his luck in England, writing and producing, which he has done ever since. He watched the rise of Ike and Tina from afar, with a mixture of regret and pride.

Throughout the early Seventies Tina consolidated her grip on rock audiences, who were swept along by her obvious class and roots, her sex appeal and up-to-date choice of material. She was all things to all men and women, and Ike slipped further into the background.

Among the many rock tunes Tina adopted and gave the Turner treatment were *Under My Thumb*, *Let It Be*, *Let's Spend The Night Together* and her other Stones' favourite *Honky Tonk Woman* which suited her down to the last sequin. 'I've always done rock because it's what I like,' she said.

'I was never really a fan of R&B. It was basically how Ike produced. But it wasn't my true taste in music. I just went totally

'I Wanna Take You Higher!' (*S.K.R. Photos*)

116

'Honky Tonk Woman'
(*Barry Plummer*)

into cover versions. I did very little of my own music.'

Tina began to develop her own skills as a writer and one of her biggest successes was *Nutbush City Limits* released on UA (UP 35582) in August 1973. But she also felt frustrated. 'I wasn't writing what I wanted. I wanted to write happy songs. Ike was a great writer, but he'd write let's say, two lines of the first verse and then he would blow the rest. So I started correcting it. I thought: "Well phooey, I can do it, I just might as well start myself." But then all I had to write about was my own experiences, about women, about reincarnation, things that I was just learning about, and that wasn't fun.'

The year before the stomping *Nutbush* became a surprise hit, and astounded critics who already thought their great days were over, Ike and Tina released the *'Nuff Said* album on UA (UAG 29256). And they came to Britain where they played a memorable concert at the Empire Pool in London, now called the Wembley Arena. As usual the show was climaxed by Tina's

119

version of Otis Redding's *I've Been Loving You Too Long*.

By now this had ceased to be an artistic triumph and was more an unsavoury routine, much to the alarm of concerned and caring critics who were fans of Tina Turner.

Geoff Brown, a *Melody Maker* critic who later edited *Black Music* and went on to *Time Out* magazine wrote of the 1972 show: 'The Turner version of *I've Been Loving You Too Long*, had evolved to include a central monologue in which Tina moaned, grunted, gasped, pleaded and rasped obeisance to Ike while he leered and murmured vulgarities in the background. Tina concluded by simulating oral sex with the microphone. Now I like my R&B as raunchy and humorous as the next person, but this had become utterly distasteful, a grotesque parody of love and downright demeaning to the singer.'

Ike's wisecracks in the background included such remarks as 'Mama don't cook no dinner tonight, 'cause Daddy's comin' home with the crabs.' When Tina sang 'I can't stop now,' Ike returned, ''Cause you ain't ready to die. . . .' When Ike and Tina finished *Lovin' You* Ike remarked to the audience, 'Well – I got mine, I hope you got yours.'

It was a fun idea which had started to go sour. Ike seemed hooked on the song, even though he didn't like Otis Redding very much, and tended to think of him as an upstart. From mere heavy breathing when they first began doing the number in 1967, it had by 1972 become, in the words of one American critic 'a complete gross-out'.

Tina explained how it had evolved: 'We cut the song and Ike kept playing the tune over and over and I had to ad lib.' Tina began to pour out any one-liners that came into her head. 'I couldn't stand there and say "Oh baby, oh baby" like an actress reading through a script without any emotion. So I had to act! . . . What I did on the Rolling Stones tour was only what had matured from the beginning.'

Tina didn't think it could go any further, and she was well aware that in New York they had called her pornographic. At the time she commented, 'I agree because like now Ike has changed words which makes it obvious what is meant. When we first started doing it, the lyrics were meant to be sensual not sexual. Sometimes he shocks me. But I have to be cool. Sometimes I want to go, "Ike, please." I start caressing the mike and he goes, "Wait 'till I get you home," and I feel like going: "Oh I wish you wouldn't say that." Everything else I feel I can put up with – but not that.'

'Shuddya face!' (*Barry Plummer*)

OVERLEAF: Filming the historic 'Soul To Soul' concert in Ghana

Tina told Ben Fong-Torres: 'But like I can't question Ike because everything that Ike has ever gotten me to do that I didn't like, was successful. I think in the early Sixties it would have really been out of bounds. Like I probably would have been thrown off the stage. But today, it's what's happening. That's why I can get by with it. Before I met Ike, I thought I'd be singing in church for the rest of my life.'

Such expressions of loyalty were laudable but wearing thin. *I've Been Loving You Too Long* was described as 'a ballad of total emotional surrender to another,' and yet total surrender was by now the last thing on Tina's mind. She had to act out her love for Ike night after night on stage, but matters were fast coming to a head.

The Revue made a trip to Ghana in 1971 to perform for the Independence Day celebrations. Other Black American performers had been to Africa before them, notably Louis Armstrong, and such visits tended to be strange experiences for the Americans. Despite the 'back to Africa' movement, contact with the ancient homeland tended to make them feel even more American. Nevertheless, Tina found it an emotional experience to see for herself the places where slaves had been housed in squalid, cramped conditions, before being transported to America in the eighteenth century. 'It was really something to see where you came from, where you began,' she said.

Tina hadn't really studied much at school and knew very little about Ghana. 'I knew nothing about Nkruma. I never did much reading. Everything I could have learned in America in two years, I learned in a week's time. I went out and toured, going a hundred miles out of the main town. I got a chance to see how the real people live, in huts, with no electric lights, and no windows. They lived in the fields.'

Tina was shocked and began to realize how little she knew about the outside world, about politics, about events, about the way other people lived in different countries. She began to read – books about the Kennedys, whose family life and glamour appealed to her, as a mother and entertainer, and about those topics which began to grab the attention of a generation previously content to be unquestioning consumers.

She took an interest in astrology and health foods. These are all-important considerations for entertainers, who are constantly on the move, forced to eat junk food and required to make daily decisions with unforseeable consequences for their careers.

It was all part of a general awakening of consciousness, a

realization that Tina didn't have to acquiesce as a silent, sleeping partner, to be shoved into the limo, and despatched post haste to the next gig, to perform on cue. Increasingly she began to sound a rebellious note in her conversations and interviews. At least there was no news black-out or censorship imposed on Tina. She was free to say what she wanted, while Ike rarely gave interviews and preferred to remain well-hidden.

If ever they appeared together, they invariably disagreed and argued. Photographs of them hugging or embracing, like the one on the back cover of their 'Nuff Said album were rare.

'Be quick, I don't do this too often,' said Ike to one photographer who asked for a picture of them together. And in fact there was no way of telling whether in the rear view 'Nuff Said shot, Ike was actually crushing Tina in his arms, or another girl sporting a long wig.

Tina, when tweaked by reviewers on the alleged failings of her voice, retorted briskly: 'I don't like any of my records.'

Somewhat piqued by suggestions that her stage act was more important than her singing she snapped: 'I don't think that much about it, because it's not really a musical thing. Oh, River Deep Mountain High was a good record. The album 'Nuff Said that Ike and I wrote . . . that's good.'

It seemed the pair were making a strenuous effort to work together. After all, with so much money at stake and so many opportunities open to them, it was the most logical and sensible thing to do. More albums came pouring out of Ike's workhouse, including Feel Good (UA UAD 29377) in June 1972, and Let Me Touch Your Mind (UA UAS 29423), the following February.

On 24 November, 1973 the Revue performed at the Odeon, Hammersmith in London, while Nutbush City Limits stayed high in the charts, and the album of the same name was released on 23 November. The album included a new studio version of River Deep Mountain High, and a version of Mentor Williams' song Drift Away.

Ike released his own solo album Bad Dreams (UAS 29549), backed by the Family Vibes, and he produced a couple of albums featuring the band on their own.

With much achieved and so much more to do, life seemed fulfilling, almost idyllic. Ike had his studio, Tina her sons. As the Seventies got underway, she took stock. 'I'd really like to settle down and spend a lot more time at home in Los Angeles, with my sons, but Ike keeps on pushing . . . We usually only work weekends now, and Ike plans to produce records for a lot of other singers, so maybe I'll be able to take a rest soon.'

The Acid Queen

The Acid
Queen

*T*HERE ARE times in any marriage when both parties need a
measure of freedom, a momentary release from ties and
responsibilities. A bolt-hole becomes essential, a place to escape,
perhaps for a few hours a week. For men there are pubs, clubs or
perhaps the luxury of a study at home or a 'den'. For women there
are usually fewer choices and options open, especially when there
are children. For a working mother, work itself becomes the only
avenue of escape.

In the best-regulated households, outlets are sensibly arranged,
and then couples can reunite with renewed fervour. The marriage
of Ike and Tina Turner, although born amidst the unpromising
turmoil of life on the road, seemed to have a good chance of

providing a firm basis for the future, a way to cool out that might lead to a more relaxed, normal life. They had money, children and a splendid rock'n'roll palace to call home. But those fiery factors in their individual personalities that had encouraged them to become performers and non-conformers in the first place, now seemed to push them headlong toward disaster.

The early Seventies were dangerous times for those who had enjoyed success over the previous few years. Fame, money and adulation were heaped on people who had set out as rebels, who despised the material world. Young idealists, and even hardened professionals, were frightened and confused by the pressures and high hopes pinned on them by eager fans. Audiences looked upon them as gods who could dispense wisdom and offer some sort of panacea.

Many suffered breakdowns or died, like Janis Joplin, who so admired Tina Turner, Brian Jones, Jimi Hendrix, Jim Morrison and Keith Moon. Sex, drugs and rock'n'roll had a lot to answer for. Even the strongest and most astute succumbed and were damaged mentally and physically by a lifestyle better called a deathstyle.

Hair grew longer but tempers shorter. Once bright, cheerful people became sullen, morose, embittered. There were so many problems and fears. Bands stayed together because of business considerations, when for their own sanity, they should have split. Marriages made as teenagers, before fame and money hit, became sources of constant vexation and misery. It might have seemed that the old saws about money not buying happiness were right. It was what the money was buying, though, that caused much of the misery . . .

Vast earnings made rock stars (and movie stars) a rich market for the drugs dealers of America. And the drug they sold most readily for the best return was cocaine. Made from coca leaves and normally used as an anaesthetic, cocaine became a fashionable rock musician's drug around 1970, when it began to be 'snorted' or inhaled in copious amounts, resulting in some users burning out their noses, and needing steel plate reinforcement.

British musicians during the Sixties had used beer, wines and spirits in liberal quantities for social enjoyment without any serious consequences beyond the odd blown-out gig and sudden acquisition of beer bellies and heavy, flushed countenances. They smoked dope, and then in the psychedelic summer of 1967, experimented with hallucinogenics, including LSD, which was then legal. 'Acid' altered the course of rock music, and produced

A pensive Keith Moon shares a 1975 interview with Tina. Keith died three years later (*Stephen Morley*)

some beautiful records and ideas. It resulted in quite a few nervous breakdowns and shattered lives too. 'Acid casualty' became the rather contemptuous name for those left semi-conscious by one too many trips.

Cocaine was more insidious in its effects: it inflated egos, shortened tempers and when mixed with 'speed' and other drugs, turned quite normal, pleasant people into monsters. Those who were fairly monstrous to start with, just got worse.

The money from the contract with Liberty enabled Ike Turner to build a huge studio complex called Bolic Sound at 1310 La Brea, Inglewood, California. Says Jimmy Thomas: 'When Ike built his studio he came off the road and decided to do just a few concert tours, now and then. But he got isolated inside his studio.'

Even United Artists were surprised at the time their artist spent thus incarcerated and a UA press release of the time commented: 'Ike, well he spends practically every waking moment at his famed Bolic Sound Studios where he dedicates himself to his music. Not only does Ike produce the Ike and Tina product, but also his own discs and those of the Family Vibes, the Ikettes and Judy Cheeks, a young protégée of his and Tina's.'

Explains Jimmy: 'Ike is a very intense person and when he goes into something he doesn't do it by half. When Ike built his studio, he wasn't at home any more. He was living in there.

'The studio was equipped with closed-circuit TV cameras, and there were four or five bedrooms. He spent thousands of dollars on it. It was like a plush, futuristic hotel. When I was on tour with Ike in Britain we met up with Terry Reid the singer. I heard Terry and his band went to Ike's studio to record and they were kept locked in there for days!

'Yeah, Ike would keep you in there like a prisoner. But anything you wanted was there. Want some chicks? What kind do you want – blonde, blue-eyed, tall, short or fat? And there were mountains of coke. It was completely over the top. I heard a guy owed him money for coke. Ike got into his car one night and shot up the guy's house. That's the kind of guy Ike was. That was his mentality, sailing too close to the wind . . .' All of this contributed to the break-up. Ike was hardly ever at home. Tina was the most patient person. She could have anything she wanted, in theory, but she didn't care about all that stuff. All she really wanted was to sing, and be with Ike and the family. But Ike had started freebasing. If you don't overdo it the hit is so good. Freebasing is smoking cocaine. It means getting a gramme of coke, breaking it down and taking away all the impurities. You may come out with

The sweat and funk goes flyin' (*Michael Putland*)

133

not much coke left. It's a pretty expensive high. If you are gonna entertain you are gonna need an ounce of this shit and it's not cheap.

'Ike was partying all the time. When he got into coke it was in a big way. Lots of guys got into coke and they were all nutters. It can change your personality. Tina never took anything. She still don't drink or smoke.'

It seemed the huge success the couple had enjoyed only fuelled Ike's appetite for excess. When Tina first met him in St Louis she noted that he never drank alcohol, and his only vices were smoking and gambling. But once they moved to Los Angeles he was drawn, like so many others, into the cocaine net. It had become a form of currency in the record business, with record companies laying it on their clients, the press and any other interested parties. Ike not only began using coke, but also took to drinking sherry and hard liquor. Tina told writer Kurt Loder in *Rolling Stone*: 'He just slowly started getting crazy. He served cocaine like wine and all of a sudden there were guns under the control board. It was like living in hell's domain.'

Hell had been creeping up on Tina, ever since her marriage, she claimed. She recalled how back in 1962 when he had taken her to Tijuana for the wedding, she had felt that it was a tawdry business. 'It was horrible. When he asked me to marry him I didn't want to because I knew then what my life would be like. But I was afraid to say no. So we went to Tijuana and a man signed the paper and he slid this paper across the desk. And I just remember it was dirty and ugly and I said to myself: "This is my wedding . . ."'

With the situation getting worse all the time, Tina found herself actually feeling sorry for Ike when he beat her up, because she knew that he was blindly hitting out, trying to hang on to his singer, to his lifeline.

It was ridiculous, but she felt guilty, and at one time attempted suicide. She took a whole bottle of sleeping pills, and planned to collapse and die on stage during a performance. But she didn't get as far as the stage. Ike walked into her dressing room and found her. She was terrified he would beat her up because he would have to cancel the show and pay off all his musicians. Tina was taken to hospital and it seemed her heart had stopped beating. Then Ike turned up at the hospital, and while she was still unconscious he began shouting and abusing her. 'You better not die, or I'll kill ya!' he stormed. Her pulse began to beat again.

Still she had to act out her love for Ike on stage night after night. *Nutbush City Limits*, the song based on memories of her upbringing, was a first tangible blow for freedom. Says Tina: 'When I wrote that song in 1973 I was writing because our "songwriter" had become schizophrenic. I had to keep doing his songs over again. It was awful. Singing all day, and writing all night. I got to hate writing. And in a sense *Nutbush* came out of all that hate. After a while I just couldn't think of anything except Nutbush, the stores and the highway and all, and so I just put it on paper.'

It is said to be good therapy to write down a list of people and things that are bugging you or causing distress, and to set fire to the list. Tina wrote a hit, not a list, but it started a fire that would eventually flare up into an explosion.

While Ike was ensconced in the studio, Tina spent her days in their house just five minutes away in Inglewood. Ike and Tina weren't wide-eyed idealists from the English suburbs. They had grown up too close to harsh realities, and Ike in particular was out to enjoy all the creature comforts that material success could buy. And he was out to impress. The pink Cadillac syndrome was applied to the décor at the Turners' home, and it had an amusing and mind-boggling effect on visitors, whether they were from the press and record industry or were friends and fellow musicians. Ike obviously believed in the dictum – if you've got it, flaunt it!

The first of many spectacles to assault the visitor's senses was a huge oil painting of Ike and Tina dressed for a wedding, adorning the foyer. Under the portrait was a white bust of the late President, John F. Kennedy, whom Tina had admired. Nearby lay an open Bible, suggesting adherence to the old Baptist ways. In the lounge was a remarkable piece of indoor landscaping, a pre-programmed waterfall, gurgling and splashing and several fish tanks, which had become something of a craze among rock musicians. In London Ginger Baker built himself a huge wall-to-wall fish tank, which eventually burst and flooded the lounge.

Near Ike's waterfall was a coffee table in the shape of a guitar. In another room a mirror in the form of jigsaw puzzle pieces was set in the ceiling, while the TV was encased in a whale-shaped cabinet.

Tina was not averse to all these off-the-wall and off-the-ceiling ideas, and expressed pride in Ike's ability to carry them out with some success. Even so, the orange carpet, green kitchen and mirror over the bed were all testaments to Ike's tastes. When Ike showed off his furnishings to Bob Krasnow, the Blue Thumb boss remarked wonderingly: 'You mean you actually can spend seventy thousand dollars at Woolworth's?'

The house was not entirely devoid of reading matter. Apart from a few sci-fi titles, Ike's books included such useful tomes as *How To Legally Avoid Paying Taxes* and *How To Scheme Your Way To Fortune*.

But the items that caught most people's eyes were the two trophies awarded Tina by Ike, each with a plaque. The first read *'To the sweetest wife and mother, Tina Turner, love's yeas, Ike Turner and your four sons.'* The other, more poignant yet, read *'To Tina Turner, the world's greatest heartbreaker. 1966.'*

With a hundred thousand dollar house and her own personal Mercedes to drive, it seemed Tina had it made. But tension and mistrust were in the air . . . Ike had installed a closed-circuit TV system at home and linked it to the one at his studio. He could sit in his office, press buttons and zoom in on any activity, any comings and goings around the rooms, foyers, and passageways. He was even able to view the activities in guests' bedrooms, with romps between musicians and groupies providing prime-time viewing.

The Bolic Sound Studios (pronounced 'bullock' in honour of Tina's maiden name) even had cameras in the men's and ladies' rooms, and the whole building had a strange, creepy air, like Orwell's Ministry of Truth. At the centre was an inner sanctum known as 'Ike's tomb' where the owner held court. This included various bedrooms fitted out with canopied beds, and a kitchen – all windowless, and under surveillance. Painted on the wall of the kitchen was a portrait of a naked Jim Brown, the football player, laying a black lady. This scene tended to dominate the dinner table underneath. A television projector and screen were also fitted, into the ceiling, to be lowered at will.

Tina disclaimed all knowledge of these fixtures and fittings and explained to visitors: 'This whole place is prepared for Ike to bury himself, if need be, for weeks on end, for recording.' Tina would be summoned from her home to the studio at any time during the day or night to help with recording. The rest of the time she would be busy with housework, cleaning, dusting, cooking and gardening.

Even before the situation between them got too serious, Ike was a hard taskmaster, demanding that Tina help him write songs, insisting she report to 'the whorehouse', each day. It didn't matter if she was feeling sick or ill. One winter Tina went down with bronchial pneumonia and her temperature rose to 104 degrees. She was rushed to hospital and packed in ice to bring down the temperature.

'The world's greatest heartbreaker' (*Robert Ellis*)

Ike came to visit her and said, 'You get out and SING, or you

137

get out of the house!' As a result, Tina was afraid to miss a show. She used a vaporiser given by a doctor to help her breathing. Willpower did the rest.

Then in 1975 came an event which got Tina out of the house and on to movie screens. Once again British rock stars came to the rescue. This time it was The Who, not the Rolling Stones. Ten years earlier, The Who's guitarist Pete Townshend had written a rock-opera, *Tommy*. After hesitant beginnings, the double album that resulted was a big seller. The music became a staple of The Who's touring show, with Pete and Roger Daltrey singing the story of a deaf, dumb and blind boy whose drug-induced expertise at the game of pinball made him a teenage Messiah. It was a strange tale, but there was no doubting the strength of the material. And rock music hadn't thus far produced much of great substance. If *Tommy* wasn't really opera, then it was certainly a powerful musical concept.

Ken Russell, one of the most brilliant, if eccentric film directors of the day, was called in to write a screenplay and direct a movie version of *Tommy*. Robert Stigwood produced the film, which starred Ann-Margret, Oliver Reed and Roger Daltrey as Tommy. Elton John played the Pinball Wizard, and there were cameo roles for the rest of The Who, notably Keith Moon as Uncle Ernie. Eric Clapton, Arthur Brown and Paul Nicholas all chipped in, but the part that ultimately proved most rewarding and memorable was that of the Acid Queen.

Tina was invited to play the Queen and she turned in a magnificent, stunning performance, that many now consider to be the best moments in a ferociously vulgar film. Tina threw herself into the role, singing with tremulous, lip-quivering power. Her demonic appearance and dramatic assault on her victim, Roger Daltrey, was in sharp contrast to the somewhat wooden performances by the other rock stars. All the more astonishing then that Pete Townshend had apparently originally earmarked the part for the ukelele-playing Tiny Tim. Instead, Tina became the hooker who dragged Tommy upstairs to her lair, to load him with drugs.

The effect on audiences was startling. Under Ken Russell's probing cameras, the singer seemed to expand and grow into a long-legged fiend. And yet she was only around five feet four.

Tina, who had so long nurtured hopes of becoming an actress was rather upset that her first role should depict her as a hooker, but she was pleased with the end result and the impact her performance made around the world. And once again she had

Rockin' through the seventies. The Hammersmith Odeon, October 1974 (*S.K.R. Photos*)

138

shown how well she could interpret a rock song with narrative lyrics.

'I was pleased with the film,' she said later. 'I always wanted to be an actress. I could act out any part as a kid. But when my first part finally came along, it turned out to be a Spanish prostitute. I kinda baulked at that. But Ken was a very convincing director.'

During her scene with Roger Daltrey she had to shove him into an Iron Maiden bristling with hypodermic syringes. 'I became so involved with it,' she recalled, 'that when I had to drag Roger Daltrey up some stairs, I literally dragged his ass up those steps. I became a madwoman. I think I scared him.'

Tina had a hit single with *The Acid Queen* when it was released on UA (UP 36043) in January 1976. The track was included on the *Tommy* soundtrack album (Polydor 2657 014) which had been issued in March 1975. Tina also made a solo album called *Acid Queen* issued on UA (UAS 29875) in October.

While it offered escape from her trap with Ike, as yet another solo success, her role as the Acid Queen also reinforced the image that Ike had helped to create and encourage. Tina Turner was the sultry she-animal, not just to the rock fans who went to her sell-out concerts, but now to millions of moviegoers. She came to dislike the image intensely, with all its painful associations. She told Steve Sutherland in a *Melody Maker* interview, 'I used to hate my image and all that I'd done with my life. I didn't like the sweat and I didn't like how ugly I looked. It was always this monster-looking face on a poster.'

Such intense feelings were bound to surface in an outburst, which led to one last beating.

It happened in 1976, while Ike and Tina were halfway through an American tour. 'Ike was feeling a little irritable that day,' she recalls. They were on their way to L.A. airport for a flight to Dallas. They had already decided that this would probably be their last tour together. Then one incident set off the explosion which blew apart their marriage as well as their business partnership. Ike offered Tina a piece of chocolate. It was melting in the heat, and Tina was wearing a white suit. She didn't relish being covered in molten candy, and with a suitable grimace registered her distaste with a cry of 'Ugh!'. Says Tina: 'He hit me with the back of his hand. I wagged my finger at him saying "All right you . . . I'm fighting back!"'

A fight began which continued all the way to the airport, with Tina so enraged she didn't even cry. 'I cursed and I yelled,' she told Kurt Loder in *Rolling Stone*. Ike protested, 'You sonafabitch,

First movie success, as the Acid Queen in Ken Russell's film version of The Who's rock opera *Tommy* (*Privilege Productions*)

140

you never talked to me like this before!' Tina raged back, 'That's right – but I am now!'

Later, when they arrived at their Dallas hotel Tina had blood all over her and her face was swollen and puffed. 'He beat me the entire way from the airport to the hotel. By the time we got to the hotel my face was swollen like a monster's,' said Tina. 'I never cried though, I laughed, because I knew I was leaving and there would be no more of this.'

But Tina still had feelings for the man who had ruled her life for so long. Exhausted by the struggle, Ike collapsed on to his hotel bed. Tina massaged him, and he fell asleep.

As Ike began to snore, Tina tiptoed away, out of his net, and ready to start a new life on her own. It would prove to be a battle in which she was hampered by all kinds of unexpected problems. But there was no turning back, no chance that the runaway would return.

There was a show scheduled in Dallas that night, but there was no way Tina was going to be there. She left with just thirty-six cents, a gasoline credit card and the clothes she was wearing. Behind her she left all personal belongings – clothes, money and property. When divorce proceedings began, and were concluded amidst rancour later that year, she asked for and got nothing, beyond her freedom.

For a while she went to live with her friend Ann-Margret, who had worked with her in *Tommy*. Tina had to live on social security – 'welfare' in America – before she could begin to pick up the pieces and build a solo career. It wasn't easy. Ike charged that she had been responsible for the cancellation of their tour, and she had to pay promoters damages amounting to thousands of dollars.

By 1977, when she first attempted to get back into the record business, fashions had changed. Punk rock was happening, and many of the older stars were being rejected and neglected. Some of the record companies didn't even bother to return her calls.

She had to get a backing band together and start going out on the road again, to help pay off her debts. A friend arranged for her to sing in the cabaret clubs of Las Vegas and Lake Tahoe. Tina launched her comeback in April 1977, with concerts in Vancouver, Denver and Washington D.C. and then unveiled her show at Caesar's Palace, Las Vegas. The reviews were good and nobody seemed to miss Ike and the Ikettes. As ragtime music heralded Tina's arrival on stage, she blasted into a selection of hits with all her old throaty power.

Agony and ecstasy (*Barry Plummer*)

'The fascination is the same, Tina is incandescent,' said the Los

Angeles *Herald-Examiner*. 'There has never been any confusion about Tina Turner's appeal. Steamy, primitive, propulsive . . .'

At Caesar's Palace she had to cut down her show to a thirty-five minutes spot, as she was only second on the bill. She wore a creamy suit and hat, which was eventually stripped off to reveal a black, sequinned leotard. Backed by four dancers, and a solid band, she danced and sang her way through the opening number *Goodtime Lady's Rag* and on into the Stones' *Honky Tonk Woman* and the ballads *Funny How Time Slips By* and *Watch Closely Now* from *A Star Is Born*. She also included a medley of rockers, a good way of packing in all the songs audiences wanted to hear, like *Jumping Jack Flash*, and *It's Only Rock'n'Roll*, while offering cut-down versions of *I Want To Take You Higher* and *Proud Mary*.

She did two shows a night, the last commencing at midnight and she was given a standing ovation each time, although the late show was usually best appreciated by a younger audience.

Out in the audience, watching the show on opening night, was Ike. But he didn't come backstage afterwards. It was only six months after her divorce and one of the most tangible signs of early success was a large billboard on the Las Vegas strip which read 'TINA TURNER', proclaiming her appearance at the Circus Maximus showroom at Caesar's Palace. Asked how she felt about seeing the sign, she said: 'I deserve it.'

Tina was also delighted at another ego-boosting announcement. She was voted one of the 'Ten most exciting women of 1977' by the International Bachelors' Society, along with Ali McGraw, Melina Mercouri, Empress Farah of Iran, and Princess Grace of Monaco. Tina thought the whole idea a lot of fun, and certainly appreciated the publicity at a crucial time.

Asked about her split with Ike she told writer Bob Lucas: 'Anytime there's a separation or divorce, there's a change, with possibilities for a whole new life in whatever direction you take. There was a certain amount of freedom, although Ike and I were together fifteen years, day and night. But there's a lot of freedom now, and I enjoy it. I've paid my dues. Even though I have help now, great people around me, I still think the same way about the performance I have to give, and I block everything else out.

'I feel that I'm not limited. There is a lot I can do and now is the time I'm going to pursue some of those things. The change is great. Now I can make it an even classier act, but always end up with what I'm known for, which is the energy and the feeling. It's important to do what people can relate to on stage. I'll always do that.'

'Thank you . . . hope you enjoyed the show' (*Barry Plummer*)

144

The show was well up to standard. After all her years on the road, this was to be expected. Tina still knew how to win over audiences. If she had any qualms about going out on her own, she didn't show them.

'Working without Ike is not that different,' she said. 'On stage I've always been out front, and Ike was directing things in the back. I've always felt I was kind of solo. Now I'll say to the band, "Give me thing" or "Let's do that," and before, Ike did that. I have to be totally in control myself and give what my emotions call for.'

Tina had prepared well for the shows. Neighbours said they could hear Tina singing *Proud Mary* early in the morning, in her home in Laurel Canyon.

Tina finished her Las Vegas stint in August then set off for shows on the East Coast and thence to Australia. It seemed there was plenty of concert work available, but her problem was how to push further and establish herself as a contemporary star and not just a cabaret attraction, tied to her old hits.

After the success of her appearance in *Tommy* she was offered several more film roles. She turned them all down, including two big movies, *Uptown Saturday Night* and *Car Wash*.

Said Tina: 'When I played the part of the Acid Queen, I took it because there was another side of being a hooker there. I got a chance to be dramatic. But since then I was offered a lot of scripts that called for hooker parts. But they weren't as strong as that of the Acid Queen. I don't mind doing a hooker part as long as it can leave a lasting impression, or have a good meaning to it. But I don't want to be typecast.'

Tina felt she would sooner do a movie like *Murder by Death*. 'I'd love to do a film like that,' she said, 'and I feel I could. Since I have my solo career I don't have to just take any part. So I'm waiting for a good script and I think now I'll get it.'

Tina was also waiting for a hit record, and in March 1979 she released her first solo album since *Acid Queen* and the split with Ike, called simply *Rough* on United Artists (UAG 30211). This was followed quickly by *Love Explosion* (UAG 30267) in September. Neither of them were big hits, nor were the singles, *Root Toot Undisputable Rock'n'Roller* and *Sometimes When We Touch* – both out in 1979. A plethora of Ike and Tina albums from the archives didn't help.

Tina took time out to think. Her sons lived with her for a while, finally leaving home to strike out on their own. Before buying a new house in North Hollywood, Tina stayed with women friends,

who interested her in Buddhism which, with its chants and
meditation, brought calm and order to her life and averted a crisis
in confidence.

Buddhism helped calm her. 'Until I started chanting, I fought
my image,' she told Brant Mewborn. 'Now I have come to accept
the sweat and wildness of Tina Turner. I used to think, "Why
can't I be like Linda Ronstadt or one of those girls who has it easy
and makes all the money? Why do I have to work so hard?"'

Tina realized, in those difficult months when she was still
treading water, that she was destined to be Tina, the high-energy,
wild woman of rock.

'That is what I'm meant to do in this lifetime and I'm at ease
with that and everything else that used to bug me. Chanting helps
get rid of all the crap in my life. It's like turning on a water hose to
clean off all the mud. When I was with Ike I was working nonstop.
It was like having to clock in. Now I'm finally getting a chance to
grow and get to know myself. Now I don't even have time for a
man!'

147

Show Some Respect

Show
Some
Respect

*I*T TOOK Tina Turner eight years of hard work, following her split with Ike, to achieve what appeared to be overnight success in the mid-Eighties. She was helped by the enthusiasm of a new manager, who revitalized her flagging solo career, and a new breed of young musicians who had her best interests at heart. They did it together, out of love and respect.

Although Tina had fought for her freedom, and feared coming under the domination of another 'Svengali', she could not carry on alone. And yet, in America she was burdened with the past: it was difficult to see how she could be brought up to date. The music scene had become ever more fragmented. On the heels of punk and the New Romantics had come Electro Pop and the increased power of producers. But Tina had seen it all before. She had worked with Phil Spector, the man who invented the idea of the boss producer, and she had conquered new idioms, singing rock songs in the Seventies when she was classified and categorized as an R&B screamer from the chitlin' circuit. Those who tried to put Tina down, should have known better. When the chance to progress came along, she grabbed it, even though she sometimes expressed her doubts and reservations.

There was no question, Tina remained an artist of arresting power and enormous potential. All she needed was the right material. There were precedents. In England, Cliff Richard, poles apart from Tina in image and roots, had nevertheless covered the same time span and shared some of Tina's problems. He was a teenage rocker who had modernized as he reached middle age, with hits like *Devil Woman* and *We Don't Talk Any More*. Coincidentally, some of his best songs on the *I'm Nearly Famous* album of 1976, had been written by Terry Britten, who became responsible for some of Tina's 'new look' songs. If Cliff could do it, so could Tina Turner.

After their divorce, Ike Turner went back inside his Bolic Sound Studios and produced some solo LPs, including *I'm Tore Up* which appeared on the Red Lightning label in 1978 and *All The Blues All The Time* on Ember in 1980. But then his beloved studios burnt down, and, shunned by the music business in the wake of Tina's revelations about their time together, Ike went to live as a recluse back in St Louis.

The first four years of Tina's solo career were spent paying off debts. The strain of constant touring and money worries meant she was unable to concentrate on writing her own new material. It seemed she couldn't follow up the bold start made with *Nutbush City Limits*.

Said Tina: 'I wasn't able to write because I felt blocked. Going through my divorce closed a lot of doors. Basically what I've experienced in my life is an R&B cliché, a lot of violence, a lot of hardship and who wants to sing about all that crap, when you've lived through it? I don't want to bring people down.'

Tina rushed into work immediately after the split with Ike, simply to raise cash, and also because it was the only thing she knew. She was helped by Mike Stewart, president of United Artists, one of the few people she could trust in the record industry. After her successful Las Vegas cabaret début there was no shortage of work. For the next few years she travelled extensively, touring America and the Middle East, and going

Tina in wide angle wig
(*Robert Ellis*)

152

153

behind the Iron Curtain to Poland.

Tina decided she needed management, to take over the business burdens. And she was tired of trying to quash the myth circulating among promoters that Tina – without Ike – couldn't really make it on her own.

'They'd always seen Ike as the motivation behind the whole show,' she said, 'the one who'd pulled the strings. I could never understand that because I was the one out there doing it. I would have had to be hypnotized not to be able to do it without him.'

Tina approached Londoner Lee Kramer, then managing Olivia Newton-John. He went to see Tina's show at an hotel in San Francisco and brought along his assistant, Australian-born Roger Davies. As it turned out, Kramer dropped out, and it was Roger Davies who became her full-time manager. Davies had managed such Aussie bands as Sherbert before leaving Australia to set up his own management company in Los Angeles in 1978. He was invited to work with Lee Kramer, who offered him an office where he could develop new talent. When Kramer left, Roger Davies became Olivia Newton-John's manager and helped revitalize her career.

Roger described Tina's show to Keith Sharp of Canada's *Music Express*: 'She was playing in this posh ballroom . . . everyone was in tuxedos . . . I thought it was going to be weird.' But Davies was impressed by the vitality of the show. He realized Tina still had great power and set about refashioning her career.

He took drastic action to update her image and started looking for a record deal. 'First we had to get rid of the band. They were all session players who wore tuxedos. We had to get some young rockers. Then we had to change the costumes and phase out the Ikette-style singers.'

This was easy enough to achieve, but it was harder to get a deal. Many of the major companies had bitter memories of past dealings with Ike. What was needed was some publicity and a modicum of excitement. Here they enjoyed swift success.

Davies booked Tina into the Ritz Club in New York for low money, with the intention of creating a buzz in the right places. It was, says Davies frankly, 'a hype'. It worked. As well as adoring fans, rock's royalty came along to cheer and pay homage. Among them were Rod Stewart, Keith Richard and David Bowie.

Rod joined with Tina to sing his hit *Hot Legs* then later asked Tina to perform on his show at Los Angeles Forum which was televized by satellite around the world to forty million viewers. Also as a result of the Ritz appearances, the Stones invited Tina to

'I can see for miles . . . !'
(*Barry Plummer*)

OVERLEAF: The British connection: Tina hugs producers Martyn Ware and Greg Walsh, clutching silver discs in recognition of a quarter of a million sales of 'Let's Stay Together'

155

sit in with them on their tour, and sing a duet with Jagger.

Tina still didn't have a record contract but Capitol Records were beginning to take an interest. Then out of the blue came an invitation to go to England. It was early in 1982 that she was approached by a team calling themselves the British Electric Foundation. They were half of the Human League, a breakaway unit which turned into Heaven 17. Producing independently as BEF, they planned an album for Virgin, called *Music of Quality and Distinction* and they wanted Tina to sing one track, the Temptations' 1970 classic *Ball of Confusion*.

The song was issued as a single, and although it wasn't a big hit, the musical collaboration showed promise and was deemed successful. The song for BEF had been videotaped at the Hammersmith Odeon and shown on MTV cable TV in America.

Capitol Records sat up and took notice. Tina was signed to the label and recorded eight tracks for them with house producer John Carter. Tina's manager thought the songs worthy but dated and too much like the Tina Turner of old. He wanted to get her to Europe and work some more with Heaven 17's Greg Walsh and Martyn Ware.

There was nothing to lose by making the trip, and Davies used an invitation for Tina to appear on Swedish TV in Stockholm as a way of getting Tina to London to record. Capitol Records were less than enthusiastic. It seems they thought Heaven 17 must be a bunch of New Wave incompetents quite unsuited to Ms Turner's style. In fact, Heaven 17 had a number of British hits to their credit and were highly respected by EMI in London.

At first it seemed Capitol's fears back in Hollywood were well-grounded. Martyn and Greg hadn't found time to write any new songs for Tina as they had been so busy with their own album. They came along to the session with a collection of their favourite R&B hits from the past. Tina was disappointed. She wanted to sing new material. 'I'm sick of that old stuff,' she announced in no uncertain terms.

A compromise was reached. Tina recorded the Al Green song *Let's Stay Together* with a new arrangement by Ware and Walsh. Ware and Glenn Gregory sang the back-up vocals. *Let's Stay Together* was a top ten hit in Britain and sold over 250,000 copies at a rate of knots. To complete Tina's delight, it was a hit in America where it was hailed as 'top dance record of the year'. Old Sixties style categories remained in force. The record was a top five hit, in the R&B charts. Sales finally topped eight million worldwide.

The heat was on. Capitol wanted a full album and gave Tina a

budget of a hundred and fifty thousand dollars, and just two weeks to pull it together. Manager and artist flew to London and began searching for songs. Capitol had selected Mick Ronson as producer, but the former Spider From Mars didn't have any material, and Roger Davies was responsible for putting together the album that grew into *Private Dancer* – in a variety of studios with a number of producers. 'It was a real hit and run situation,' he said later.

It was planned to use David Bowie's song *Tonight* on the album, but David used it as the title track of his own album. It was replaced by another Bowie composition *1984* and in the meantime David invited Tina to sing on his version of *Tonight* when he recorded it in Canada.

Mark Knopfler of Dire Straits came up with Tina's title track *Private Dancer* which he had written while recording in New York. The lyrics were rescued from a scrap of paper left in the studio. *I Might Have Been Queen* was a biographical song for Tina composed by Jeannette Obstoj, producer Rupert Hine and Fixx guitarist Jamie West-Oram – who also played on the track.

Two of the best cuts on the album, which turned out to be a bouquet of hits, were *What's Love Got To Do With It* and *Show Some Respect* both by Terry Britten, a friend of Roger Davies' from Australia. Tina disliked both songs when she heard the demos, but grew to like them as she sang and worked out on them in the studio.

It was a whole new learning experience for Tina, working with different producers, and English rock musicians. The album was completed in around three weeks. It went triple platinum.

Tina set off for a European tour that was already scheduled. When she arrived in London to play at The Venue in December 1983, she found a great wave of excitement had begun to break. During the next two years, Tina enjoyed a succession of hits with songs from *Private Dancer*. Her electrifying version of Ann Peebles' unusual *I Can't Stand The Rain* was a number one smash in America and the singles helped keep the album on the charts until it sold around five million.

Some diehard soul fans thought Tina was going too far into the pop field. It didn't matter. It was more important that her voice be challenged by interesting material, rather than be burned up on basic funk riffs.

Private Dancer gave her superstar status at home and abroad. In Los Angeles, the Mayor declared 6 July, 1984 'Tina Turner Day'.

But as her new career took off with meteoric speed, Tina and

This fantastic, feathery creation was one of several costumes used by Tina on her 1978 tour, seen here at the Hammersmith Odeon in February (*Robert Ellis*)

OVERLEAF: Lionel Richie welcomes his special guest on tour (*Relay Photos*)

159

her manager found they had a string of commitments – made when times were tougher.

After recording with Bowie in Canada, Tina flew to Memphis to start a tour supporting Lionel Richie. He had specially requested her presence. This was no chore. Tina was delighted at the chance to play just as the album was coming out, and the exposure helped its sales *and* boosted *What's Love Got To Do With It.*

There were some sixty dates to play and a band was put together with members of Dire Straits to back Tina. It wasn't easy for her. It was the first time she had been on stage without the backing of massed singers and dancers and she had to carry the show on her own.

'It was real hard being on stage by myself at first,' said Tina. 'Lionel's crowd is not my crowd. And I was singing brand new material and the only thing they wanted to hear was *Nutbush City Limits, Let's Stay Together* and *Proud Mary.*

But as Tina persevered with her new songs and radio stations began playing the album, the public got the message. It wouldn't be long before she was touring again, but this time as the headliner.

The Lionel Richie tour had been a sudden windfall. Less welcome was a contract to play at eighteen McDonald's hamburger conventions. Some critics thought this well below her dignity, and painted a lurid picture of drunken employees falling about while she tried to perform. It was no worse than the chitlin' circuit and the salesmen loved her. Roger Davies had contemplated cancelling the tour, as the album climbed higher up the chart. The dates had been booked when Tina's organization were still trying to earn enough money to pay the wages.

McDonald's reaction was swift. 'Fine – we'll sue,' they said. Tina played the dates.

But she dropped out of another pre-hit project. Yorkshire Television, a British commercial TV station, had planned to make a programme about Tina's life. Work began during her visit to London in 1983, but eventually had to be stopped as Tina's management cooled towards the idea.

Yorkshire TV had given the job to one of their top directors, James Cutler. He recalls what happened when he wanted to make a programme about one of his favourite singers. 'We had a terrible time. I had been working on a very serious documentary about the Windscale nuclear plant and as light relief I was given a different assignment. We were going to make a documentary about Tina.

'It was to be a look at her life story, the way she had split with

Ike Turner, and her life at forty-three, still on the road. It would
have been a gritty documentary about one of the greatest
performers of all time. I had always been a fan of hers, right from
the days when she toured Britain with the Rolling Stones in the
Sixties. I don't think she realizes how great she is!

'She had started to make a comeback a couple of years ago, so
we thought it would be a great idea for a documentary. But she
"came back" too soon. Before the documentary could be made,
she had a hit record, so the management regarded it differently. I
can understand why. They didn't want that kind of documentary
any more, just a free plug on TV. She had an unexpected hit with
Let's Stay Together and they wanted to forget about the struggles.
They didn't need that kind of TV show.

'I think they were wrong. European audiences would have
wanted a chance to see her story. But they were not interested,
they wanted a pop profile and it fell through.'

(Eventually Tina was featured in an American pop documentary
series *Legends* which concluded with the narrator saying, 'Tina
Turner may have given offence to some people over the years but
she is a true legend.')

Added Cutler: 'We filmed her in concert at The Venue, and
were only allowed one handheld camera and no tripod and we
weren't allowed backstage. We were forbidden to film her going
into the studio because she wasn't in her make-up. I felt we had
been misled and we spent a lot of money on the project. I met Tina
later at the BBC. Although the project had been discussed for
months and letters sent to the management and filming had been
done, Tina didn't know anything about it, and she didn't know
why the cameras had been pointing at her. She knew nothing
about the documentary. But there were no bad feelings, and I
wished her good luck.'

Tina had more pressing engagements. While she was in
London, she was interviewed on TV and mentioned her
long-nurtured desire to be an actress. Watching the show was film
director George Miller. He was in the throes of planning the third
Mad Max film, to be called *Mad Max Beyond Thunderdome*. He
was searching for someone to play Aunt Entity in his story of life
in the Australian desert after the cities have been destroyed in a
global, superpower conflict. Mad Max the hero was to be played
once again by Mel Gibson, whom many hailed as the new Clint
Eastwood. This series of violent but exciting films had been hugely
successful, and sparked off a whole new genre.

George Miller had been considering asking Jane Fonda to play

Aunt Entity, the ruler of a town which struggles to exist in the aftermath of war and destruction. But he had begun to see the role as a Tina Turner-style character, and finally flew to Los Angeles to catch up with Tina and give her a screen test. She passed and in November 1984 Tina joined George and the crew in the northern wastelands of Australia to start filming.

She had to endure intense heat and dust and cope with the demands of learning lines and getting action sequences right. There was no audience to work to, only the cameras and technicians.

Tina had her hair shaven to make room for an appropriate wig, which went with the atomic-chic punk outfit favoured by the all-powerful Aunt, a sort of chainmail mini-skirt. Tina was so excited by the story and the action, she wanted to do the most dangerous stunts herself. A double was used instead, and she contented herself with cheering at the sidelines.

Nevertheless, as a 'warrior woman' she thought it a great chance to play herself, an extension of her rock'n'roll image. 'It was a pleasure for me to guest in Mad Max,' she said later. 'The director George said I could do it, and he got the performance out of me, although it took time for me to settle into it.'

She had a tendency to gabble her lines, as her high tension energy spilled over into her acting style. 'It was an exciting part, very strong, very physical, but it was straight drama. I had never done that before. Mel Gibson was great, a real rock'n'roll actor. All that leather! He is beautiful and cute as well. He really helped me sink into the part.'

Mel as Mad Max, defender of victims of post-apocalypse terrorism, gave Tina much moral support. 'When I first went onto the set, I was terrified,' admitted Tina. 'Mel helped me tremendously, although I still found watching the rushes every day nerve-racking'.

Said Tina: 'I had been watching horror movies, like *The Exorcist* and *Conan* and that is what I wanted to do, be totally inhuman, a fantasy figure.'

The soundtrack music for the film, released as an album, contained a song by Tina *We Don't Need Another Hero*, written by Terry Britten and Graham Lyle. It was a hit single in August 1985.

Also that summer Tina appeared in the historic 'Live Aid' concert organized by Bob Geldof to raise money for famine relief in Ethiopia, and she played more dates in America and Canada. The pressure was on for her to rush out another album but it was decided that Tina needed a rest, after two years of almost

The Wig That
Conquered the World
(*Barry Plummer*)

164

continuous touring, recording and filming. There were fears that she might suffer from overkill, and disappear in a pop scene that was going through pop idols at an alarming rate.

'There's no financial pressures right now and Tina needs a rest,' said her manager. 'The important thing is to pace her properly and record songs that reflect her abilities as a well-rounded vocalist and not just a screamer.' Roger Davies thought this had been achieved on *Private Dancer*. The plan was to make the next one, due in 1986, even better.

'Tina feels that she can record for at least the next five years. Then she'll be fifty and after that . . . well, we'll see.'

Meanwhile the world was beating a path to Tina's door. As her records soared she was hemmed in by reporters and pursued by fans. She enjoyed all the attention, but there were times when people became too pressing. Shouting, 'Oi look – it's Tina Turner!' inches away from her face while she was out shopping, was one way to earn a withering glare.

She created an aura around herself so that just a look was sufficient to warn off the unwelcome. Most of the time she bubbled with laughter and fended off the inevitable questions, about Ike, about the lean years, about her family and her religion. She celebrated her hits with an unashamed spending spree. Her manager lent her his American Express Gold Card and she set off for Harrods and other fine stores. With fur coats and a Rolls-Royce she was a self-made woman whose real life story was better than any romantic, soap opera fiction. Tina undoubtedly had the last laugh.

As the tempo of life increased, sleep and a chance to be alone became more precious even than the fruits of a successful shopping expedition. She escaped to a new all-glass home in Sherman Oaks, California, which she shared with a live-in friend, her pet cat Maxi. Although there were rumours of a liaison with a young businessman aquaintance, Tina damped down stories of her finding a new husband or boyfriend.

'It's a bit too soon,' she said. 'I am just learning about people and enjoying it. I never thought my career would be so interesting.'

Her British fans hoped that as she had enjoyed success first in the UK, she might consider a local chap – *any* local chap. 'I'm really grateful to Britain,' she said, 'and to British fans for their support, but I have never dated a British man. I would have to have a very strong man. I would not want to mother him. When I was married to Ike, he told me to do that.'

After sixteen years of marriage, she'd had enough of acting as

166

Come up and see me
sometime (*Paul
Cox/LFI*)

unpaid manicurist and hairdresser. There was no evidence to
suggest she was in a hurry to marry anyone. She told Karen
Spreadbury:

'I've been single for eight years and it has been the greatest time
in my life. It seems I spent all my life married and I knew nothing

167

of any other possibilities. I don't even miss the company either, because I'm having such a wonderful time. I am so much more confident now. I am afraid that another relationship would spoil my way of life. So I'm not looking for one.'

As time passed, Tina had first attempted to blot out her memories of the old days. It was only when pressed that she had lifted the veil over the darker aspects. Once past the first burst of anger, she began to play down the stormier side of her relationship with Ike, and cherish the happier times.

'It was a normal, everyday marriage,' she said, 'and I look back on it now as a phase in my life.' She even allowed that she too might have been a tyrant as a young girl. She hadn't entirely abandoned Ike and felt sorry for him as his career took a plunge. She even made a brief appearance on one of his last solo albums, *The Edge*.

At the height of her newfound fame, the last thing she wanted was to be embroiled in any more rancour or bitterness. 'Everybody thinks I've been struggling,' she said. 'In fact I'm having a great time! I just can't believe it's all been happening, and so fast!'

After two years of unprecedented popularity and deeply satisfying achievement, Tina was in no hurry to make hard and fast pronouncements about her future, but was ready to take pride in the story, thus far.

'I don't want to jump out of singing,' she said, 'but I've been doing it a long time, so I think there is a way to bow out gracefully and slowly, to travel less and continue to record and then do movies.'

Her success had made her a hero of Women's Liberation, but Tina told Geoff Brown: 'It seems that I live a woman's liberated life but I was not aware of it because I'm not into movements. I was just surviving. That is the kind of woman I am. Everyone just puts a label on you as soon as you get successful. So I have to be real careful. It's really not easy at the top. My God! They're coming from every angle. Come and do this, why can't you help us do that? I'm only trying to help myself, hold on a minute.'

Tina laughed at the idea of becoming another hero, whatever the cause. But in her more serious moments she felt only pride and gratitude.

'It's an honour to be accepted, and I have no regrets about being a legend and still being around. But you can't do what I did being negative. I don't think I'm a strong black woman who made it. I feel I'm a wonderful person who made it!'

Hit singles, albums, movies . . . what more d'ya want?

168

'Simply
the Best'

'Simply the Best'

ROGER DAVIES had helped Tina find the right new musical direction that would take her away from the Las Vegas circuit and out into the wider world of Rock'n'Roll. Within a few years the good looking Australian had helped her escape from the music biz preconceptions that had held her in check. He had also built a brighter, safer world to help Tina blot out the past. His approach, which was one of care and understanding, was in total contrast to all she had endured at the hands of Ike Turner, who had ruled her life to the point where she had even had to ask permission to leave his side.

In a video documentary *Tina Turner: The Girl From Nutbush*, Tina recalled her last days with Ike before the final bust up. 'I hated the songs, the pictures of me were terrible, and I didn't like my life. That was my existence, but I made the best of it. It got me where I needed to go. There was a time when Ike and Tina couldn't get arrested, we couldn't get a hit record, and we couldn't get any airplay. We couldn't write rock music because that wasn't our life style. We'd just do our current single and everything else was covers. Ike was a smart man, very cunning and he did well for himself, until he started doing drugs.'

Tina remembered the effect heavy use of cocaine began to have on Ike's personality. 'Dates were falling off and Ike was getting more and more insecure. He couldn't get a hit record and I was being blamed for it. When I was singing in the studio, I wasn't singing what he wanted me to sing, so I was the reason he couldn't get a hit! I had to leave because he could have killed me. He believed I was the cause of him not being successful.'

The now notorious fight in the car on the way to Fort Worth, Texas, which triggered the break up, was the first time Tina had hit back. 'It frightened him. I couldn't go on stage anyway, because my face was disfigured. We had fought all the way to the hotel. I felt good about fighting back. When I got to the hotel, I was almost laughing. I knew that I was walking – I was out of there. It was the Fourth of July, Independence Day, 1976.'

Tina had gone to a nearby Ramada Inn for sanctuary and the manager offered her a room for the night. Friends recalled that Ike searched everywhere. He couldn't believe she had left him. He refused to cancel any of their dates, which exposed them to legal action when the act failed to turn up.

Tina hinted at the hardships she endured in the early days following her escape. 'I had people shooting into my house, cars burned, threats . . . my life was in danger.' But when she began to build her career on her own she discovered she had at least learned something useful from her time with Ike.

'It's common knowledge that Ike took everything – but he didn't. I'd learned how to *survive* with Ike. I'd learned how to cover songs and work without a record hit. I knew I could always work because I'm a performer. But then I realised what I was missing was proper management. I wasn't going anywhere. I could have been in Las Vegas for all my life.'

Roger Davies had a plan: 'What we had to do was get her back in the public eye.'

Tina knew she had to take a hard look at her image before she could launch into the rock world. 'I am extremely critical of myself. I became what I am from looking at all the old film footage of myself. I corrected myself often, the facial expressions, the way that I stood, all of that was to make myself better. The critics said I had turned my back on my old music, but I'm more successful now than I've ever been in my life, so who is right, and who knows what's best for me?' With a glamorous new image, new stage moves and first class musicians to back her, she was on her way to becoming a stadium rock attraction. A posse of British rock star friends gave a welcome impetus to her manager's hard work.

The Rolling Stones in particular had fond memories of the energy and soul of the Ike and Tina Turner Revue on their tours together in the Sixties. Keith Richards was ready to offer practical help following Tina's show at The Ritz Club in New York in December 1982. It was the night that David Bowie signed to EMI-Capitol. Roger Davies got a call from Capitol to say that sixty people from the company wanted to come down and see Tina. They were throwing a party for David and he wanted to see his favourite female singer.

Accompanying Bowie was Keith Richards. After the show they went back to the Stone's suite at the Plaza Hotel with Tina. Richards began to play the piano, David and Tina started to sing and Ronnie Wood joined in on guitar. 'They jammed for hours. It was a crazy night!' recalled Roger. 'Around 7 a.m. as we were going home, Keith asked Tina if she would do some shows on the next Rolling Stones tour. That's when the momentum started.'

The British connection continued with the partnership of Craig Marsh and Martyn Ware, who produced the hit version of *Let's Stay Together* and *Private Dancer*. Davies was justifiably proud of their achievements with the album. 'It sold over ten million copies and we got five Grammys from that album. We had five top ten singles in America, and Tina's first ever number one single with *What's Love Got To Do With It*.'

If Tina Turner had contemplated resting on her laurels after the success of *Private Dancer* she showed no sign of it. Throughout the Eighties her career blossomed, her prestige rose and her life was celebrated in an authentic film biography. Even as her fiftieth birthday beckoned, she continued to tour, packing out stadiums around the world with a spectacular show that was light years ahead of her old cabaret routines. She amazed audiences and press with her boundless energy, as she danced and sang her way through gruelling two hour shows.

Excellent, well produced albums stormed the charts, providing a succession of hit songs. Her voice remained a vital, vibrant instrument, steeped in soul and blues, although some complained it was Adult Orientated Rock.

'The songs that I sing now have to relate to a young rock audience,' explained Tina. 'Can you imagine me singing blues about cheating on my husband to those kids? Kids can't relate to that. They want to hear fun things. Rock'n'Roll is fun. It's full of energy and laughter. To me a lot of Rhythm and Blues songs are depressing. They're about a culture and a way of life. Rock'n'Roll is white basically and because white people haven't had that much of a problem, they write about much lighter and funnier things. Because I didn't get depressed about my life, I happened to like songs that weren't depressing!'

Pacing her work, living in harmony and enjoying new found inner peace, Tina was ready to face fresh challenges. Her stamina was astounding but she joked: 'Just like a mother is always tired, a singer is always tired. I suppose if I was honest, I could use five years off!' She had barely taken a day off from the music business since she was a teenager, and by the mid-Eighties, the demand for personal appearances was overwhelming. She responded with more tours, one-off shows and prestige events.

Tina caused a sensation in Brazil at the Rock In Rio Festival in January 1985, when she appeared alongside Rod Stewart, Queen, Whitesnake and AC/DC. At the 27th Grammy Awards held in February *What's Love Got To Do With It* was voted Record of the Year, Song of the Year and Best Female Vocal Performance. *Better Be Good To Me* was hailed Best Female Rock Vocal. In March she played ten sell-out shows at London's Wembley Arena, as *I Can't Stand The Rain* hit the charts, peaking at number 57.

In June *Mad Max: Beyond Thunderdome* was released and her performance as Aunty Entity won her a Best Actress Award from the NAACP. Her success led to further film offers. However she turned down a part in director Steven Spielberg's film *The Color Purple* because she felt it was too close to her own real life experiences.

On July 13 she was invited to sing at the historic Live Aid concert in Philadelphia, where she joined her old mate Mick Jagger in a raunchy duet on *It's Only Rock'n'Roll*. Mick later said that Tina didn't mind what he did while they were singing, whether it was snatching a kiss or smacking her bottom. But she invariably took her revenge by treading on his feet in her high heeled shoes.

Europe greeted the revived Tina with an enthusiasm she did not always enjoy at home. 'The Americans didn't like her that much,' explained Mick Jagger. 'They always compartmentalised her music.' But Germany proved a staunch ally and during her 1985

When I'm cleaning lampposts – getting close to the fans (*Laister Dickson Ltd*)

177

European tour, eight German dates had to be increased to thirty to cope with ticket demand.

It was at this point that America began to change its mind, and realise it was missing out on a phenomenon. Tina was delighted when she heard that *We Don't Need Another Hero (Thunderdome)* from *Mad Max* had reached Number Two in the US Top 100 singles chart. She enjoyed another hit when *It's Only Love*, a duet with Bryan Adams, got to 29 in the UK singles chart in November, and breached the US charts in January 1986.

Tina had been playing in Vancouver, Canada, when Bryan tried to get in touch with her to tell her about the song. He passed the message on to her management and they invited him to meet her. 'I got a 'phone call back asking me to come and see her show,' said Adams. 'Afterwards I was escorted into a room full of journalists and Tina walked by everybody to tell me: "I love the song!"'

There were more superstar collaborations to come. In June 1986 Tina sang at the Prince's Trust concert in London, sharing the bill with Eric Clapton, Elton John and Bryan Adams. They steamed into a powerhouse version of *Tearing Us Apart*, with Phil Collins playing drums. Another highlight of the show was Tina's duet with Paul McCartney on a spirited version of *Get Back*. It was the first time Tina had met Paul – he gave her a big hug and said: 'Finally, we meet.'

Tina was thrilled at playing with so many great names in rock and said: 'You know what I felt like? I felt I was the only girl in the playground with the guys. I was out there with the guys, playing ball!'

While her personal 'star' was being embedded on the Hollywood Walk of Fame outside the Capitol Records Tower in Los Angeles, Turner was busy preparing her next album, *Break Every Rule*. The title would have a special significance for her. 'I'm a farm girl and I have worked to get what I want. I wanted to sing. I wanted the star on my door, to be all of what I had seen in the movies when I was young. I went against the rules, I made the rules for my life – but I never let go of the dream.' She remembered the days when as a school girl she had had to pick cotton. 'And I *hated* picking cotton!'

The first single from the album *Typical Male* was a big hit in America, where it reached number two, and the UK where it got to 33 in the chart. The album topped charts in nine countries and went platinum in America where it sold over a million.

In March 1987 Tina began her exhausting twelve month *Break Every Rule* world tour, in Munich, Germany. She tried to

Tina Turner's Spectacular R&B Extravaganza! (*Laister Dickson Ltd*)

178

convince everyone it was going to be her farewell. The tour would break box office records in thirteen territories. As she sang her way round the world she visited 25 countries, some for the first time in her career. She played 230 concerts to more than three and a half million people, while singles culled from the album including *Two People* and *What You Get Is What You See* continued to dominate the charts.

In August the package, sponsored by soft drinks giant Pepsi Cola, reached America, bringing her fresh acclaim at home. Her appearance in a brash Pepsi TV commercial reinforced her image to millions of viewers around the world.

The whole shebang reached a spectacular climax in South America, when she played before 182,000 people in the Maracana Arena, Rio de Janeiro, Brazil, in January 1988. The event went down in the Guinness Book of Records as the largest audience ever assembled for a single performer. 'How do you follow that?' she later asked. 'You don't. I realised my dream and anything that happens now is a bonus.' The tour finished with a concert in Osaka, Japan. It was calculated she had played to some four million fans during the whole astonishing exercise.

As Tina came off the road to rest and recuperate, a double album, *Living In Europe*, was released which did well in Britain, but only just scraped into the US album chart. May of that year saw a video, *Rio '88*, of live footage from Brazil.

In the wake of such massive international success, money poured in for the girl from Flatbush. America's *Forbes* magazine reported in a survey of top entertainers' income that Tina Turner had earned £150,000,000 during 1987–88. In 1989 she announced she would retire from touring. There were no longer any obvious financial reasons for her to continue such a gruelling life style.

Tina was at the peak of her career, but her old partner was not enjoying the best of luck. In July 1988 Ike Turner was sentenced to a year in prison for possession and transportation of cocaine. Determined to continue his musical activities, he began recording an autobiographical album called *My Confessions* for release on the Starforce label. The following year however, he further incurred the wrath of the law for drug offences and began a four year prison sentence in California's San Luis Obispo Men's Colony. In January 1990 he was convicted in his absence of driving under the influence of cocaine, although the Santa Monica jury was deadlocked on two felony cocaine charges, forcing a mistrial. In August 1990 he threatened to sue Tina Turner for $70 million on his release from his four year sentence. In an interview he said: 'I

Although shy in person, Tina can pout perfectly for a camera (*Laister Dickson Ltd*)

181

read that Tina made $35 million. That isn't really her name. The name Tina Turner belongs to me.' He added that Tina's claims he had beaten her were exaggerated. 'I beat her no more than the average guy beats his wife.'

But in another interview from prison, Ike expressed regret at what he'd done and blamed his downfall on drugs. 'A lot of the things I did, I regret that they happened. I can't undo the past – but I'm sorry.' He hoped for a reconciliation but there was little chance of that ever happening. Tina dreaded the thought of their meeting again.

18 September 1989 saw the release of Tina's third studio album on Capitol, *Foreign Affair*, which yielded a powerful hit single *The Best*. Featuring a distinctive sax solo by Edgar Winter, the song would be a favourite choice for TV and radio commercials over the next few years. The song was a Top Twenty hit in the US, stayed in the UK Top 10 for four weeks, and was Number One in seven European countries.

Four of the songs on the album were written by Memphis based songwriter Tony Joe White, famed for such hits as *Polk Salad Annie* and *Rainy Night In Georgia*. Tina was pleased and surprised at the success of the collaboration, on which she gained her first credits as producer and arranger.

The album tracks included *Steamy Windows, The Best, You Know Who (Is Doing You Know What), Undercover Agent for the Blues, Look Me in the Heart, Be Tender With Me Baby, You Can't Stop Me Loving You, Ask Me How I Feel, Falling Like Rain, I Don't Wanna Lose You, Not Enough Romance* and *Foreign Affair*. The album went straight to Number One in the UK albums chart and topped charts all over Europe.

Reviews were encouraging. Said one critic: 'It's an admirable feat of longevity that Tina Turner still survives as a credible pop star. *Foreign Affair* won't let anybody down. It's a continuation of former glories, bridging the generation gap with simple, well orchestrated songs and powerful performance.'

The album's gestation period began when Tina was in Hollywood with Roger Davies looking for suitable movie scripts. They had decided not to make another album until 1990. Recalled Tina: 'The movie thing just wasn't happening. We thought, maybe we should just go ahead and make another album.' Tina was concerned that at this stage in life she couldn't risk being off the scene for too long. 'Once we had made that decision it was amazing how quickly the songs came in. It was like we had said to the gods, "Give us some songs." And they said "Okay, here you are!"'

Almost an unguarded moment (*Laister Dickson Ltd*)

182

Tony Joe White's arrival on the scene proved fortuitous. Although Tina had tended to fight shy of blues material because she found it 'too depressing', she was delighted at Tony's ability to mix R&B themes with clever lyrics. His contribution would help set the mood and pace of the whole album. Said Tina: 'I was thrilled. I bet The Rolling Stones would have loved to have done those songs!'

It was no sweat for Tina to deliver the blues with feeling – it came from her roots. 'I just had to sing in my natural voice.'

When Tony met Tina he was puzzled that she kept laughing at him. 'I was worried that my fly was undone or something.' Eventually Tina explained the cause of all the hilarity. She told him: 'I thought you were a black man!'

While Tina was pleased at the way *Foreign Affair* came together it still rankled that she could not get the movie part she wanted and that Hollywood didn't seem ready to accept her as a serious actress.

She made lots of promotional videos but regarded them as 'rehearsals' for the acting roles she would have preferred. She had made a great impression as the Acid Queen in *Tommy* and Aunt Entity in *Mad Max*, yet movie moguls (or at least their administrators), still categorised her as a singer, and the opportunity to develop her screen acting talents was largely wasted.

As if to emphasise the point, that summer Tina recreated one of her earliest movie roles, when she once again played the part of the Acid Queen in a stage version of The Who's rock opera at a charity event in Los Angeles.

On 26 November 1989, Tina Turner celebrated her fiftieth birthday with a lavish, star studded party at the normally sedate Reform Club in London. It was attended by many old friends, including Eric Clapton, Mark Knopfler, Bryan Adams, and Duran Duran's Simon Le Bon. There were video messages of congratulations sent by David Bowie, The Rolling Stones, Annie Lennox and Dave Stewart. Tina arrived with her German boyfriend Erwin Bach, wearing a £25,000 Christian Dior gown, trimmed with silk flowers, and was greeted with the spectacle of a huge birthday cake, topped with a crown and flanked by two iced lions. It was over the top, and she loved every minute.

The same month she was invited to sing in front of the Queen and Prince Philip at the Royal Variety Performance Show at the London Palladium, assuring critics that she wouldn't 'tone down her performance'. Tina appeared in a blue mini-dress and sang

Wouldn't you buy a used T-shirt from this person? (*Laister Dickson Ltd*)

184

Steamy Windows from *Foreign Affair* and was praised for delivering the most dynamic performance of the night.

British newspapers raved: 'Tina, who will be fifty on Sunday, was the sexiest star on stage. Her raunchy routine managed to outshine Janet Jackson, even though she's less than half Tina's age.' The *Daily Mirror* proclaimed that she had 'stolen the show'.

Now she had reached middle age, Tina again insisted that she wanted to give up live work and complained: 'People don't believe me when I say I have retired from the stage, but I have been performing for 28 years without a break, and that's it! I want to do movies. I am ready for them. I'm not shooting for an Oscar but for the experience of being an actress. I've always been able to sing but I've always wanted to act. On stage I act out Tina Turner, so it's just a matter of being directed for the camera.' Unfortunately there were few suitable parts for a black actress that didn't involve science fiction or period dramas. Rock'n'Roll beckoned once more.

A *Foreign Affair* European tour was announced in November, and 150,000 tickets for a show at England's famed stately home, Woburn Abbey, sold out within days. Tina complained at the thought of yet another bout of heavy touring. 'I just don't want to do a big tour again,' she told reporters. 'It's too exhausting. I don't want to travel. I've done all that. The dilemma for me is that there is such a buzz about this album I feel I have to do something just for the fans. That's my attitude. But – no hit, no show!' She admitted she had to bow to pressure. 'Fans kept asking me why I didn't want to sing the songs on the album, so I decided OK – I'd do some dates.'

Some found her prickly attitude intimidating. She explained: 'I have found men pretty threatened by me because I am independent and strong. I am not a wimp in any way. I call myself a Man–Woman. I've got a man's short, muscular body and a woman's long legs. I usually get rid of my men after two and a half years.

'I hate men who are submissive. I like a man to be firm with me and know how to handle me. I've always admired British men – they're so charming. The British people have such good brains.'

Just before Christmas 1989 Tina had a health scare. She had discovered a lump which it was feared might be breast cancer. After suffering weeks of anxiety, she was given a clean bill of health. She went to see a cancer specialist at a West London Hospital and after an exploratory biopsy it was confirmed that the lump was benign. A cyst was later removed in a 90-minute operation.

When did string vests ever look this good?
(*Laister Dickson Ltd*)

Musically however she continued to flourish. The hits kept flowing and the third single from the album, Tony Joe White's *Steamy Windows* reached number thirteen in the UK charts in January 1990. By March *Foreign Affair* had already outsold *Private Dancer* in the UK and attained multi-plantium status in fourteen different countries.

The *Foreign Affair* tour, sponsored by Pepsi Cola, began in Antwerp, Belgium in April 1990 and finished in Rotterdam, Holland in November. At Antwerp's Sports Paleis she was greeted by 18,000 cheering fans. Tina came on stage in a skin tight black leather outfit with tails, changed into jeans, and then wore the stringy, see-through mini-dress she had worn on the cover of the album. Her choice of songs spanned her entire career, and included *The Best, I Don't Wanna Lose You, River Deep Mountain High, Proud Mary, Nutbush City Limits, Private Dancer, Let's Stay Together* and *What's Love Got To Do With It.*

The show featured spectacular special effects, including lasers, fireworks and flame jets which cost over £2,000,000. Tina made her grand entrance, Busby Berkeley style, in a blaze of lights, fireworks and smoke from the top of a massive 30-step illuminated staircase, to the tune of *The Best*. Deafening explosions made her band wince during a pyrotechnical display that accompanied her *Mad Max* song *We Don't Need Another Hero.*

One of the biggest tours of all time, it beat records set by the Stones, Bowie and Elton John. The statistics were impressive. Tina played some 125 shows at 65 stadiums and 60 arenas, reaching 3.5 million people in 19 countries.

An entourage one hundred strong, including bodyguards, a personal assistant and a masseuse, travelled the globe with Tina, together with musicians, sound and light technicians, riggers, truck drivers, electricians and carpenters. Each night the stage had to be erected at a different venue, in a gruelling eight hour operation, followed by an overnight journey to the next town with all the equipment packed into thirteen articulated lorries. As Tina finished the last notes of *Be Tender* at the end of each concert, it was the signal to rush for the exit. Tina swept away in her Mercedes past police escorts, heading for the sanctuary of her hotel suite.

During the European part of the tour she played at the Palace of Versailles in France on 28 June, becoming the first woman artist to do so.

MEE-OW
(*Laister Dickson Ltd*)

Hours before her show in front of 40,000 fans, the police considered cancelling the event, as heavy rain had turned the area into a mud bath, churned up by the arrival of the equipment trucks. A detachment of 200 French soldiers helped get the trucks on to the site by building a special metal track. The show went ahead and climaxed with a dazzling firework display. In July, she made her first concert appearances in Britain for three years and caused pandemonium at box offices. The UK tour commenced on 14 July with five shows at Birmingham's National Exhibition Centre on 14, 15, 17, 18 and 19 July. Another scheduled show at the 30,000 capacity Gateshead International Stadium on Sunday 22 July sold out in five days, and an extra date at the North East's biggest venue was added for Saturday 21 July. 'My British fans have been so good to me over the years that I wanted to do some more shows to say thanks,' she explained.

Another rock-starved region of Britain succumbed to Tina fever. It was announced she would play a special concert at Ipswich Town football ground in East Anglia. Some 24,000 tickets sold out in four days for the show on 25 July.

The first of her five shows at Birmingham NEC were given good reviews, although male and female critics alike seemed to squirm at the idea of a mature woman remaining both sexy and dynamic as a Rock'n'Roll performer. There were constant references to grandmothers, and the age of the audience, as if this were somehow relevant. The *Independent* chose to call her a 'prize fighting goldfish', and concluded, 'She is powerful, dynamic, dominant and she appears to go on forever. Not the kind of thing men admit to finding attractive. Not in public, at least.'

The *Daily Telegraph* had a problem with the use of an extending crane arm to project Tina on a platform 40 feet over the heads of the audience. 'It was one of the most pompous stage shows in living memory. Only Tina Turner could get away with it,' sniffed their reviewer, apparently unaware similar mechanical devices were in common use at the better class of pop show.

A female critic in the *Guardian* seemed to think that nobody in Tina's audience over the age of thirty could possibly appreciate her sex appeal, but suggested that most of her fans were actually 'fifty something'. Press pictures of crowd scenes showed her audience consisted mainly of twenty-five year olds.

Pursuing the ageist theme the *Daily Mail*'s Spencer Bright wrote: 'Tina is everyone's favourite grandmother . . . after the Queen Mother. She's a few years younger of course, at 50. Despite her grand rock age, her physical strength is undimmed. She can still put on a gruelling act that leaves audiences almost as breathless as the performers.' As for Tina singing *Better Be Good*

How to have fun and keep warm on a photo shoot (*Laister Dickson Ltd*)

190

To Me suspended from her 'chariot', said Bright: 'It was all ridiculous and over the top, but so what? It was still an exhilarating tonic.'

Britain's sober *Financial Times* offered a more spirited defence. Wrote Antony Thorncroft: 'Anyone who thinks there is something voyeuristic, even tacky, about a Tina Turner show would be quickly disillusioned. It is brilliant entertainment. Rarely have I seen artist, band and audience so freely enjoying themselves. If she thinks this is her farewell tour she will need to be visited by the heavy mob.'

At her Gateshead show she was watched by 60,000 fans who paid £30 a ticket and were thrilled by her dynamic dancing. A few days later on Saturday 28 July, Tina sang at Woburn Abbey to an estimated crowd of 50,000. Once again demand for tickets had been so strong she had to play a second sell-out show the following day. Throughout it all she was accompanied by her regular band, with James Ralston (guitar), Jack Bruno (drums), Tim Capello (sax), Ollie Marland (keyboards) and Kenny Moore (organ and piano), who had been on the road with Tina for ten years. The Princess of Wales was among those who graced Tina with a private visit. Elton John, Mark Knopfler and Kate Bush also came to pay their respects.

In December Tina was back in the chart, duetting with Rod Stewart on a remake of a Marvin Gaye hit *It Takes Two*, the theme of the latest Pepsi Cola TV commercial. Tina and Rod rehearsed the song over a telephone link, and recorded tracks separately, Rod in Los Angeles, Tina in London.

At the beginning of 1991 the old partnership of Ike and Tina Turner was honoured when the pair were inducted into the Rock'n'Roll Hall of Fame. Neither attended. Ike was in prison and Tina was resting after her tour.

Later in the year a greatest hits CD compilation, *Simply The Best*, was released and went to Number One in the UK album charts. It topped the charts in twelve other territories, and sold over four million copies. As well as songs from her recent past, it included three new ones, *Love Thing*, *I Want You Near Me* and *Way of the World*. Top London club producer-mixers CJ Mackintosh and Dave Dorrell added a new version of Tina's 1973 hit *Nutbush City Limits*. Phil Spector also remastered and equalised the classic *River Deep Mountain High*, for its first appearance on CD.

The compilation, accompanied by a best selling video, was the pinnacle of a comeback hailed 'the most amazing in music

Even on a video shoot Tina gives her all (*Paul Cox/Laister Dickson Ltd*)

history'. It was confirmed that since the release of *Private Dancer* in 1984, Turner's worldwide record sales had topped 25 million.

In July 1992 Tina signed a new recording deal with Virgin Records in America and in November she began work on a new album to coincide with the release of the motion picture story of her life, *What's Love Got To Do With It*.

Some years earlier, the Walt Disney company had bought the rights to Tina's autobiography, *I, Tina*, written with co-author Kurt Loder. Filming had begun towards the end of 1992 and Tina was asked if she would rerecord some of her old Ike and Tina Turner hits for the soundtrack.

'To be honest, the thought did not thrill me,' said Tina. She hadn't sung some of the numbers for two decades, but when she found her backing band enjoyed working out new arrangements, she joined in the spirit. 'Their enthusiasm rubbed off on me. It was surprising to hear how well most of the songs withstood the test of time.' Among the older numbers was a raunchy version of BB King's *Rock Me Baby*, Tina's own composition *Nutbush City Limits*, the Johh Fogerty hit *Proud Mary*, Ike Turner's *A Fool In Love*, and the stomping *Shake A Tail Feather*.

She also cut three new songs for the soundtrack. Among them *I Don't Wanna Fight*, was written by Steve DuBerry and Lulu. Said Tina: 'This was a song which I feel perfectly summarised a large part of my life. It seemed like the ideal theme for the film.' She also sang Bryan Adams's *Why Must We Wait Until Tonight*, co-written with top producer Mutt Lange. Terry Britten and Graham Lyle contributed the title track and *Stay Awhile*. The film, with Angela Bassett in the title role, was well received. Tina made a brief appearance as herself in the last moments of a well acted drama that was packed with superb music. The film told the often violent story of Tina's life with shocking realism, while capturing the humour and excitement that were also an integral part.

She had been invited to serve as a consultant on the project, but freely admitted she was not entirely enthusiastic about the job. Said Tina: 'I wrote *I, Tina* as a response to all those people who at the biggest, most exciting time of my life, when my solo career was taking off, kept asking me about Ike. I thought, "Is this guy gonna come back and haunt me forever?" I don't think I would have told that story otherwise. It was a pretty disgraceful life, but I lived it, and other people have lived it as well. I think it helped a lot of women make decisions about their lives and maybe changed a lot of men's attitudes about how they treat their women. But I never thought I would have to relive it again in a film.'

She made it plain that she hadn't wanted to play the title role. 'I played that part too long in real life and never wanted to do it again.'

The movie traced Ike and Tina's career from their first hit *Fool In Love* to the point where she finally gained the courage to leave the man who had beaten and dominated her for most of her life. Just the mention of his name was enough to cause her pain, years after their split. 'I still hear from him. He still tries to get in touch with me, although that doesn't mean I have to accept his calls.

'You have to learn to forgive and forget and I have, but I don't ever want to see him. He needs help. When I was around, I tried to help him but couldn't so I finished it. I gave sixteen years and all of my money and it's over now. I rebuilt myself, so I am through with all of that.'

Said a British friend: 'When Disney bought the rights to *I, Tina* she probably thought they wouldn't make the film until she was 90 years old. She didn't expect them to do it so quickly! She still hasn't seen the film to this day. She has cut that period out of her life and blanked it off. She is desperate to act but the film people only send her parts as a downtrodden women.'

With so much of her success coming from outside the States, Tina spent five years living in London. She looked at houses for a year before eventually buying a large six-storey town house in Holland Park which she dubbed 'The Eiffel Tower'. But she only stayed there a year before moving to Cologne to buy a house closer to her boyfriend, German record executive Erwin Bach. She also sold up another home in Los Angeles as she completed her move to Europe. 'I lived in America all my life and grew tired of it. I was attracted to Europe by the way of life, the eating habits, the culture. It's beautiful. I moved to Cologne because I was in love.'

She denied that Erwin was a playboy. 'He's a young-old man, just like I'm a young-old woman. That's why we get on so well. We laugh and always have fun. He's not the marrying type and doesn't want children. We live together and that's enough. Men have never made me happy, but my life had changed. I think this relationship is the best I've ever had in my whole life.'

Tina admitted that in the past, as a struggling woman, she may have been reaching out for a man's help. 'I might even had got it mixed up with love. Now I only need a man for his love and attention. I can take care of myself. When I look back on my life and all the physical abuse I suffered, I still have no regrets. I've learnt something from every step of my life.'

Tina has confirmed that a ten year commitment to Buddhism

helped her a lot. 'It changed my attitude to life. I don't get upset or stressed. I take things very easy. Even through the hardest times I think I laughed, even in my worst moments. I don't take life so seriously.

'If you believe that things are gonna get better, you can laugh your way through and shed some light in the darkness. That's what I figure it's all about. I believe I've touched upon something about living a free and happy life in my practice of Buddhism. I'm not afraid about it all coming to an end one day. I've learned a bit about death and I will welcome it when it comes. Buddhism made me aware of the fact that each of us as an individual is responsible for what happens to us, no one else.'

During 1993 Tina decided to undertake her first American tour for six years. 'She's had more retirements than Frank Sinatra!' was the affectionate cry. She began the *What's Love Got To Do With It* tour in Reno, Nevada, in July and continued across the States to Canada and on to Australia, and Japan. The tour finished in New Zealand in November, just three days before her birthday. She decided not to tour Europe and planned to spend 1994 relaxing and buying a new home in the South of France. Her relationship with Erwin Bach remained steady and despite occasional remarks that she wouldn't mind having another child, there were no more children. She had four sons she had cared for: Ike's two sons by Lorraine Taylor, Ike Jnr, and Michael; Tina's son Craig by Raymond Hill; and the son Ike and Tina had together – Ronnie.

Love has remained a constant theme throughout Tina Turner's career, in songs if not in life. She did not always find love as a young, unwanted child, and was denied it in a brutal marriage, but she certainly found it in the hearts of millions of fans. She found affection too, from those close to her in business and later in life she found greater understanding from her mother. What's Love Got To Do With It? was the question. As the roars of applause echo down the years, the answer must be . . . everything.

Jamming . . . literally
(*Paul Cox/Laister Dickson Ltd*)

*Tina's
Hot Wax*

Tina's
Hot Wax

*I*T IS often claimed that a natural performer's best work cannot be captured on record. An artist like Tina Turner, it is said, is best heard in a 'live' situation, at a concert, or preferably in a club. It's an argument that has long been applied to jazz musicians, who are supposed to produce their most creative work at 3 a.m. in smoke-filled rooms.

As a young singer, first groomed by Ike Turner, she sang from the heart and soul with the accrued experience of generations of blues shouters, and inspired by the new idols of the day, in particular Ray Charles. Unless the recording equipment was filled with cement, or the engineer suddenly taken drunk, there was no reason why the power of Tina's voice and her personal magnetism

shouldn't shine as brightly on record, as it did on stage.

In the early Sixties, when Tina first began recording with Ike, the experience of being in a studio was a novelty, and a challenge. With just three minutes to make a mark, and a couple of 'takes' to get it right, studio discipline spurred Tina to even greater efforts. She sang at full bore as her first two singles *A Fool In Love* and *It's Gonna Work Out Fine* testify. Indeed, for many fans these two tracks remain among the most riveting and satisfying of her career, not to be equalled for many years.

In the days when record output was strictly limited, there was always the feeling that the best performances, the best work was hidden away in the vaults. But when thousands of 'out takes' and alternative versions of many jazz and blues records began to become available in the de-restricted Seventies, it became clear that in many cases, the originals were the best. The three-minute masterpiece, made with minds concentrated by the hands of the studio clock, could still beat all the hours of on-the-spot recording, not to mention the stuff that had been discarded by impatient record companies, in the first place.

It is the case that while Tina has been hailed for her work in a spectacular cabaret setting, on record, she has always performed best when her fire and energy have been contained and directed.

Tina sounded better on the studio sessions than on subsequently released, live albums from the early years. It was the hit singles that helped establish the Ike and Tina Turner Revue, and gave financial support to the whole concept of a touring show with dancers and singers. The vocal interplay with the Ikettes on *It's Gonna Work Out Fine* gave useful support to Tina. When she ran out of wind at the end of a phrase, particularly in the lower register, there was Mickey Baker ready with a response and the Ikettes chanting the hookline as a safety net.

When singing without any other vocal support, Tina can sometimes display an erratic sense of timing, particularly with difficult lyrics that don't scan very well. It is part of the charm of her ballad performances that you can never be quite sure which way she is going to go, as she soars high up the scale, teeters for a while, fades, as if disappearing into wispy high-altitude clouds, then swoops down to earth again. Hearing Tina on slow, emotional tearjerkers, is just as exciting as listening to her blitz through an uptight, highspeed soul stomper. She's like a pilot carrying out an aerobatic display – wings flashing, engine screaming.

Tina in her hours of triumph at Wembley, London, March 1985 (*Adam Scott*)

Tina has at her command a whole armoury of growls, grunts, snorts and screams, ready to be interjected into the bloodstream of

203

a song. In her early days she used these devices with gay abandon, out to shock and sock it to 'em. But by 1969, just a few years after the raucous savagery of *A Fool In Love*, she could take a song like *(You've Got) Too Many Ties That Bind* and deliver it with considerable restraint, at least until the final rousing bars!

The early Sue recordings by Ike and Tina all had a groovy innocence, epitomized by the 1963 boogie tune *Gonna Find Me A Substitute*. While not exactly a great song it was the kind of goodtime performance that knocked them out on the chitlin' circuit. The hardcore soul is there in *Sleepless* from 1961, when she sounded like a scalded wildcat. Undoubtedly, Ike must have had his hands full in those formative years, and must have taken cognizance of the old couplet: 'A woman, a dog and a walnut tree, the more they're beat, the better they be.'

Tina's answer to this kind of attitude was expressed in the pre-women's lib outburst *Dear John* from 1966, which showed that at least Ike and Tina could laugh about their fussin' and feudin'. All these tracks can be explored on the compilation album *Tough Enough* released in 1984 and put together by blues and soul expert Cliff White.

The album *The Ike and Tina Turner Show* referred to in Chapter Two has been reissued several times, most recently on Edsel ED 152. These 1966 live recordings do not show Tina in a good light. She sounds too harsh and masculine on *Finger Poppin* and a shade breathless and brutal on *Let The Good Times Roll*. In the heat and battle of hard-touring it was obvious that Tina's voice was being over-worked and distorted. She got the cheers – and at the time it probably seemed very exciting – but in the long term, it was a waste.

She blitzed through standards like *You Are My Sunshine* and *Twist And Shout*, delivered with great savagery, while the band shimmered rather than rocked, led by Ike's grooving guitar. As the rest of the girls joined in, you can feel the tension building with that mysterious alchemy that only Black American artists can ever achieve, no matter how hard the rest of the world tries.

For all my strictures on Tina's style as evinced by the 1966 showtime recordings, the raw energy and brazen attack Tina displayed on *Something's Got A Hold On Me* remained awe-inspiring. The same cannot be said of *Tight Pants* – a crude reworking of *High Heel Sneakers*. Sang Tina, doubtless at Ike's behest: 'Put on your tight pants baby, put your toupée on your head.' It was pretty grim stuff, best forgotten. It only served to underline the contention of many critics that Ike didn't really know how to use Tina other than as a battering ram.

Wrote Richard Williams in his book on Phil Spector: 'Ike . . . a very tough, foxy guy, he had choreographed their act right down to the exact pitch of Tina's every wail and the last unison pelvic twitch from the Ikettes. But he never really understood how to get her across to the huge white audience of that era.'

It was on the basis of shows like the one recorded at the Skyliner Ballroom, Texas, that a record industry pundit could say: 'Ike and Tina weren't very highly thought-of, then. They were just an R&B act who couldn't cross over.'

When Ike found it difficult to get a hit in the battle for the elusive 'cross-over' from black to black *and* white audiences, he wasn't above getting Tina to re-fashion an earlier triumph. This is the case with *Hard Times*, a song which appears on *The Soul Of Ike and Tina Turner*. It sounds like a mixture of *A Fool In Love* (complete with similar backing vocals, and cries of 'Woah woah, yeah, yeah') and with the lyrical ideas of *Dear John*.

Throughout the mid-Sixties, Ike and Tina churned out an endless series of sides, some inspired, some workmanlike, others tired and devoid of ideas, like *Flee Flee Flee* with its listless tenor saxophone backing.

During her years with Ike, Tina was often called on to try her hand at everything from country songs to cocktail ballads. Throughout it all, while sax players and brass sections did their worst, Tina always delivered, and willingly re-vamped *A Fool In Love* yet again as *Am I A Fool In Love*, and letting Ike try out *It's Gonna Work Out Fine* as a 'new' song called *Something Came Over Me*. This came complete with grumbling verbal attacks, spoken with undisguised bitterness, presumably this time by Ike, which

205

lacked the whimsical wit of the original version.

All this smacked of desperation, and it was no surprise then that Ike should agree to let Phil Spector have a go at producing Tina in 1966. *River Deep Mountain High*, when heard in context against a background of stuff like *Something Came Over Me* and *Tight Pants* is a revelation.

For all Spector's celebrated faults, at least Tina was being treated right. The chain of endless R&B ditties and re-cycled riffs was broken. She had a chance to shine with an unusual song crafted by Jeff Barry and Ellie Greenwich in collaboration with Spector. The dramatic, rumbling introduction, the pause for Tina's cliffhanging vocal introduction, and the romping beat combined with Wagnerian orchestral backing resulted in a unique record, one of the finest of the period and still revered.

Tina's vocal prowess was fully stretched and given a kind of Grand Canyon setting. It was no wonder people raved about the record even when it looked as though it might nosedive in England – but for the dedicated promotion of Tony Hall. His battle to get it played on radio brought the desired results. Fewer people in England had heard Tina's past work, and so they had no preconceptions. As far as most record buyers were concerned the sound of *River Deep Mountain High was* the sound of Ike and Tina Turner. Alas, on the album of the same name, not all the material could match the first flush of brilliance. Indeed, *A Love Like Yours (Don't Come Knocking Every Day)* was a stilted, embarrassing exercise, and the return of yet another re-make of *A Fool In Love* sounded almost like an admission of failure, with Tina having been given her fling with Spector, and now being dragged back to Ike's domain. You can almost hear Tina's disappointment, as she belts out the lyrics 'one more time'.

There were a few more successful Turner-Spector collaborations in the can which were included on the album. *Hold On Baby* was an echoing hoe-down also written by Barry and Greenwich, as was the excellent *I'll Never Need More Than This* with unusual chord changes. Although reminiscent of Shirley Bassey singing a James Bond theme, it was another chance for Tina to stretch out and show her astonishing technical ability and range.

A touch of schoolgirl opera experience was revealed in this epic, somewhat spoilt by duck-quacking noises from a demented baritone sax player allowed a few unfortunate bars. This was a 'what might have been' exercise, for the rest of the album was padded out with more ordinary Ike and Tina material, produced with less flair than Spector but with more professionalism – which

A new era dawns. Greetings to the eighties (*Barry Plummer*)

206

means that twenty years on, they sound less dated than 'the wall of sound'.

Somehow, the vocal challenges Spector was able to fling at Tina had to be combined with a more sophisticated backing than either Ike or Phil could provide. Tina had to wait several years before that dream could be fulfilled and pop music itself had grown and learnt many a painful lesson.

To his credit, while Ike maintained the working basis of the Revue, between *River Deep* in 1966 and the start of the Seventies, he brought many good rock songs into the act for Tina to turn into hits, like Creedence Clearwater's *Proud Mary*, the Beatles *Come Together* and the Stones' *Honky Tonk Woman*.

Tina's voice and style didn't change that much over the years, except that she smoothed out some of the rougher growls and seemed more in control. On Warner Brothers' live album from 1969 *Ike And Tina* (K 36001) it was clear she was still called on by Ike to work up a lather. *You Are My Sunshine* had a fanfare of note-splitting trumpet players, and she choked her way through the gospel-style wedding day lament *All I Could Do Was Cry*. The latter was a biting, ironic performance only Tina could deliver with all her maniacal power. It's impossible not to choke back a tear on hearing this today! Tina the actress was born during such nightly routines, a mixture of dialogue and song with its roots in both the Southern Baptist church and vaudeville.

It was with the album *'Nuff Said* that Ike and Tina moved more convincingly out of the chitlin' circuit Sixties and into the Rockin' Seventies. Here at last was good production and a clean sophisticated sound, courtesy of Ike's brand new Bolic Sound Studio. Cuts like *I Love What You Do To Me* and the shouting *Baby (What You Want Me To Do)* were blessed with trumpets that could play in unison, in tune, and with rhythm sections powered by the recently-liberated bass guitar. Playing standards had risen dramatically. Young session players had such a command of their instruments that they could bring new sharpness and accuracy to soul.

Not all the songs on *'Nuff Said* were brilliant, but even the slow and somewhat plodding *Sweet Flustrations* (the 'l' is not a misprint!) had an improved quality that shone out like a beacon after the muffled rumblings, and twitchy beats of the Sixties.

The new reliance on mid-tempo funk grooves was typified by *What You Don't See (Is Better Yet)*. All these titles revealed Ike's amused exploitation of the voyeur instinct: part of the pleasure was putting the sex symbol on display and then snatching her back from the eager hordes. What you got was a black eye.

'Nuff Said was however a fine production job by Ike, and a great leap forward. It sounded as though they were having fun, especially on the 'Nuff Said instrumental jam with Ike on electric organ. Incidentally, the organ sounded anachronistic on *Tell The Truth*. It also tended to hiss rather badly, notably on *Pick Me Up (Take Me Where Your Home Is)*.

The influence of *Proud Mary* could be detected in *Moving Into Hip Style – A Trip Child* – which suggested that Ike was encouraging Tina to sing more rock'n'roll, a topic liable to set them off on rows about who did and didn't want to get into rock.

It was undoubtedly good stuff, and Ike was hard at work with an endless outpouring of competently produced albums, from *The Hunter* through to *Nutbush City Limits* which burst upon the scene in 1973 and yielded their classic hit single. Here at last Tina was singing about something other than love, fickle menfolk and thinly-disguised tales of life with Ike. It was a shortlived burst, but there came another chance to break out, with Pete Townshend's marvellous composition *The Acid Queen* from his rock opera *Tommy*.

As she sang the number from the soundtrack of Ken Russell's *Tommy* movie, Tina interpreted the lyrics with a dash and conviction that made it one of the finest performances of her career thus far, better perhaps than *River Deep* and certainly better recorded. Her voice shone through, above the spirited backing of a bunch of English rockers. The results augered well for the future.

She was backed by a wildly-thrashing Kenny Jones (depping for Keith Moon) on drums, Ron Wood on guitar, (instead of Townshend), John Entwistle on bass and Nicky Hopkins on piano.

If 'Nuff Said and Nutbush City Limits had seemed brighter by far than her pre-Spector recordings, this was like a searchlight. At last she was free of the riffing bass and tight-assed rhythm sections. The loose craziness of the young rockers seemed to give her more freedom to do battle with the song. She wasn't pushed into breathless repetition but encouraged rather to tackle the lyrics in her own time and on her own terms.

It was another taste of what could be done without Ike, even more successfully than with Spector. Her final, cackling bursts of laughter, so effective in the movie, as she did vile things to Roger Daltrey, were also a sign of her own joy. What a shame Tina didn't record a whole album of Townshend songs, although this might have proved embarrassing for The Who's regular lead singer.

It wasn't long after the 'Acid Queen' experience, and her performance in the film that Tina finally split from Ike. Even then she didn't take the risk of teaming up with a young rock band, and when she went out on the road again, it was with the old-style backing.

Tina recorded an *Acid Queen* album in 1975 and a few more tracks with Ike which were issued on *The Edge* in 1980 and again on Tina Turner *Mini* on Fantasy (MPF 4520) in 1984. The tracks included Bill Withers *Lean On Me* which was certainly soulful, but like *Shame Shame Shame* with Ike's clipped guitar riffs, was a slip back in time.

Other cuts from these last sessions with Ike, recorded around 1976, included the powerful *Only Women Bleed*, one of her best recordings, technically and lyrically. These middle-period cuts showed Tina totally in command, full of experience, technically able to flip her way around a difficult narrative with unstinting attack. *Only Women Bleed* was too heavy for radio audiences used to a diet of mindless pap, but Tina made even a mumble sound eloquent.

Philadelphia Freedom was impassioned, fiery and timeless, another example of the consistency Tina brought to all her work. Good or bad, Tina always made a song sound brand new.

But all her hard work was not to be diffused for ever on riffs with blatant put-down titles like *Use Me*. After a couple of false starts with her own solo albums came *Ball Of Confusion* with BEF and then *Private Dancer* – the album that was the consummation of all her years of hard work and experience. It was ten years after *Acid Queen* and eighteen years since *River Deep Mountain High* but it was like the winking of an eye. Tina was reborn with *Private Dancer*.

The opening cut *I Might Have Been Queen* set the mood of determination and defiance. A fine song by Jeannette Obstoj, Rupert Hine and Jamie West-Oram, it encapsulated Tina's story. 'I'm a soul survivor,' she sang, 'I look down and I'm there in history.'

From here on the album just flowed, like Michael Jackson's *Thriller* an expression of confidence and inspiration. It didn't matter how the songs had been scraped together and the sessions slotted in hastily. Despite the changing background of musicians, producers, writers and studios, a sound, a *feeling*, permeated the whole work, giving it cohesion and direction.

What's Love Got To Do With It by Terry Britten and Graham Lyle had a touching, wistful quality lacking in most of Tina's years

Sheer sex (*Paul Cox/LFI*)

210

of fighting and flaunting. She could still stomp and roar, as on *Show Some Respect* which had the jumpiness of *Nutbush City Limits* in addition to the spartan clarity of Eighties' technology. Composer Britten played guitar on this one and added backing vocals.

Most extraordinary of the *Private Dancer* songs was *I Can't Stand The Rain* with a nagging, milk-bottle-rattling riff emanating from the keyboards. Tina acted her way through the Ann Peebles' song with unusual close to the chest vocals, contrasted by

A hard act to beat – Grace Jones and Tina share a hoot (*Gary Gershoff/LFI*)

212

bellowing, trumpet-style guffaws. Some hated and mocked the song, but it was brilliantly conceived, and a risk well worth taking.

Private Dancer was in total contrast, and perhaps the first song in thirty years Tina had sung 'straight' without a hint of a scream or a whoop, at least for the first chorus before a burst of exuberance for the line about 'American Express will do nicely – thank you!'

This was very much a rally round by Tina's British chums. Written by Mark Knopfler of Dire Straits, it was performed by some of his own lads, assisted by Jeff Beck and sax player Mel Collins. Never had Tina sounded so relaxed, so cool.

Side two was also rich in delights. *Let's Stay Together* with non-macho vocals by Glenn Gregory and Martyn Ware seemed to heighten Tina's sensuality more than all the 'Use Me' jive of yesteryear.

Better Be Good To Me by Mike Chapman, Micky Chinn and Holly Knight spread out with Jamie West-Oram's sympathetic guitar chords and Rupert Hine's keyboards which leant more to progressive rock in the Yes mould than bar-room funk. With Trevor Morais' stomping drums, the tune seemed to develop just as much excitement as in the old days of the Revue.

Tina showed once again her amazing ability to chew up a mouthful of tricky lyrics on the fast moving, heavy metal rocker *Steel Claw* with Jeff Beck once again burning strings, hotter than he had on record in many moons.

And just to bring more lumps in the throat and tears to the eye, Tina sprang from the boisterous burn-up on *Steel Claw* into an emotional reading of Lennon and McCartney's *Help*, sung slow and funky. On this, (the only non-British backed cut), she was accompanied by the Crusaders.

The album was brought to a climax with David Bowie's *1984* – a version flawed only by the use of a drum machine, throbbing stiffly. Trevor Morais should have been used on this cut, and maybe in the future it could be re-recorded with a proper drummer.

Private Dancer set new standards of excellence both for Tina and the mainstream of pop music. She kept the momentum going in 1985 with another hit single *We Don't Need Another Hero (Thunderdome)* sung with a strangely low key spooky intensity that perfectly suited the character she portrayed in the film *Mad Max: Beyond Thunderdome*.

In 1986 came another superb album *Break Every Rule*, which yielded a brace of hits including *Typical Male* featuring Phil

Collins on drums, then at the height of his 'Mind if I sit in mate?' period. Curiously enough, Tina seemed influenced by Collins the singer in her vocal delivery, and there is a strong flavour of mid-Eighties Genesis about the piece. A version of Robert Palmer's track *Addicted To Love* also from the album was another hit and an example of Tina's effortless ability to cross over into pop rock. Its easy, laid back beat gives Tina a chance to sing without screaming while retaining a tremendous sense of soulful blues power. When a piercing sax solo takes off however, she can't help but hit a few high notes of her own! The album showed Tina getting back to her roots, perhaps in response to a ground swell of opinion among critics and fans, or more likely, from a desire to put her career into personal context. She wanted to see how far she'd come and whether she could still cut it with the less sophisticated material of yesteryear.

As well as the well crafted pop songs, she tore into two old favourites, *In The Midnight Hour*, and *Land of a Thousand Dances*, both worn out in the Sixties, but here revived and refreshed.

In the midst of a flow of apparently effortless pop hits, critics carped that Tina was sometimes in danger of losing her depth of expression and sense of involvement with a lyric. They only had to listen to her stirring, heart stopping performance of *Be Tender With Me Baby*, one of the highlights of *Foreign Affair*, her 1989 blockbuster, to hear that she'd lost none of her ability to turn men's legs to jelly.

All facets of love and passion dominate the mood and spirit of a richly satisfying collection of songs which include the throbbing *Steamy Windows*, a Tony Joe White vignette inspired by memories of teenage love sessions in the back seat of a Cadillac.

Both these milepost studio albums showed that Tina's vocal prowess and technique had matured and mellowed with age and experience, while her ear for a good song ensured she always had material that either stretched or excited her to produce simply the best performances. As the world couldn't get enough of her, a successful collection of concert performances was released in 1989, *Live In Europe: Tina Turner*; this was virtually a celebration of her career, kicking off with the anthemic *What You Get Is What You See*, and including dynamic versions of *Break Every Rule*, *I Can't Stand The Rain*, *Addicted To Love*, *Proud Mary*, *Nutbush City Limits*, and *River Deep Mountain High*.

Another collection of highlights from her studio album *Simply The Best*, (1991) included eighteen of her finest chart busters. These emphasised the range of emotions unleashed and explored by her voice, haunting sadness, vibrant exuberance, aggression and compassion are all displayed with a versatility and confidence few artists can match.

What's Love Got To Do With It, her 1993 album, accompanied the film of her life story, and included the telling *I Don't Wanna Fight*, written by Steve DuBerry and Lulu, which seemed to perfectly sum up her philosophy now that she had achieved most of her aims in life.

One of her finest vocal outings on the album, which delighted her oldest fans was a raunchy version of the BB King song *Rock Me Baby*, a rare trip back to the blues for a singer who began her career listening to BB King records on the radio. A new version of *Nutbush City Limits* sounded a shade brittle and lacked the bite of the original, but Tina and her team did great things to other old favourites like *Proud Mary*, *A Fool In Love* and the stomping *Shake A Tail Feather*, all designed to relive the spirit of the far-off Sixties.

With her latterday recordings Tina managed to achieve an amazing balancing act. She kept faith with her roots and adapted to changing music fashions without sounding as if she was trying too hard to be modern, often the fate of her contemporaries, whose own careers had passed their 'sell by' date.

Songs like *The Best*, and *What's Love Got To Do With It*, delivered with power and passion, keep Tina Turner at the forefront of the world's rock stage way into the 1990s.

Even when the day comes when the dancing has to stop, the voice of Tina Turner will still have the power to bring both pleasure, optimism and joy in an ongoing celebration of the human spirit.

Discography

Ike and Tina Turner Singles

A Fool In Love/The Way You Love Me
November 1960 London HLU 9226

*It's Gonna Work Out Fine/Won't You Forgive
Me?*
October 1961 London HLU 9451

*It's Gonna Work Out Fine/Won't You Forgive
Me?*
(re-issue) February 1964, Sue W1 306

The Argument/Poor Fool
August 1964 Sue W1 322

I Can't Believe What You Say/My Baby Now
November 1964 Sue W1 350

Finger Poppin'/Ooh Poop A Doo
January 1965 Warner 1B 153

Please Please Please/Am I A Fool In Love?
May 1965 Sue W1 376

*River Deep Mountain High/I'll Keep You
Happy*
May 1966 London HLU 10046

Tell Her I'm Not Home/Finger Poppin'
July 1966 Warner WB 5753

*Anything You Wasn't Born With/Beauty is
Just Skin Deep*
August 1966 HMV POP 1544

A Love Like Yours/Hold On Baby
October 1966 London HLU 10083

Goodbye So Long/Hurt Is All You Gave Me
October 1966 Stateside SS 551

*Somebody (Somewhere) Needs You/Just To
Be With You*
November 1966 Warner WB 5766

I'm Hooked/Dust My Broom
March 1967 HMV POP 1583

*I'll Never Need More Than This/Save The Last
Dance For Me*
September 1967 London HLU 10155

So Fine/So Blue Over You
April 1968 London HLU 10189

We Need An Understanding/It Sho' Ain't Me
August 1968 London HLU 10217

*River Deep Mountain High/Save The Last
Dance For Me*
January 1969 London HLU 10242

*I'm Gonna Do All I Can/You've Got Too Many
Ties That Bind*
April 1969 Minit MLF 11016

*I'll Never Need More Than This/A Love Like
Yours*
May 1969 London HLU 10267

*Crazy 'Bout You Baby/I've Been Loving You
Too Long*
July 1969, Liberty LBF 15223

Come Together/Honky Tonk Woman
February 1970 Liberty LBF 15303

Make 'Em Wait/Everyday I Have To Cry
March 1970 A&M AMS 783

The Hunter/Bold Soul Sister
May 1970 Harvest HAR 5018

I Want To Take You Higher/Contact High
June 1970 Liberty LBF 15367

*Proud Mary/Funkier Than a Mosquita's
Tweeter*
January 1971 Liberty LBF 15432

River Deep Mountain High/Oh Baby
February 1971 A&M AMS 829

Ooh Poo Pah Doo/I Wanna Jump
June 1971 UA UP 35245

I'm Your's/Doin' It
November 1971 UA UP 35310

*Crazy 'Bout Baby/I've Been Lovin' You Too
Long*
(re-issue) January 1972 UA UP 35219

Feel Good/Outrageous
June 1972 UA UP 35373

Let Me Touch Your Mind/Chopper
October 1972 UA UP 35429

*River Deep Mountain High/A Love Like
Yours/Save The Last Dance For Me*
(re-issue) February 1973 A&M AMS 7039

Born Free/Work On Me
July 1973 UA UP 35550

218

Nutbush City Limits/Help Him
August 1973 UA UP 35582

Fancy Annie/River Deep Mountain High
March 1974 UA UP 35632

Sweet Rhode Island Red/Get It Out Of Your Mind
May 1974 UA UP 35650

Sexy Ida – Parts 1 & 2
October 1974 UA UP 35726

Baby Get It On/Baby Get It On
(disco version) July 1975 UA UP 35766

Delila's Power/That's My Purpose
October 1975 UA UP 36028

Ike and Tina Turner EPs

The Soul of Ike and Tina Turner
1964 Sue 1EP

The Ike and Tina Turner Show Vol. 1
1965 Warner WEP 619

Somebody Needs You
January 1967 Warner WEP 620

Sue Session
October 1983 Sue ENS 1

Ike and Tina Turner LPs

The Ike and Tina Turner Show
April 1965 Warner WM 8170

Greatest Hits
November 1965 London HAC 8247

Finger Poppin'
July 1966 Warner WB 5753

The Ike and Tina Turner Show
(re-issue) July 1966 Warner 1579

The Ike and Tina Turner Revue
July 1966 Ember EMB 3368

River Deep Mountain High
September 1966 London HAU 8298

The Ike and Tina Turner Show
Vol. 2 February 1967 Warner WB 5904

Greatest Hits
June 1968 Hallmark HM 563

So Fine
January 1969 London SHU 8370

Outta Season
June 1969 Liberty LBS 83241

In Person
October 1969 Minit MLS 40014

Ike and Tina's Greatest Hits
December 1969 Warner WS 1810

River Deep Mountain High
(re-issue) March 1970 A&M AMLS 971

The Ike and Tina Turner Show
May 1970 Valiant VS 118

Come Together
August 1970 Liberty LBS 83350

The Hunter
September 1970 Harvest SHSP 4001

Workin' Together
February 1971 Liberty LBS 83455

The Fantastic Ike and Tina Turner
March 1971 Sunset SLS 50205

Her Man His Woman
June 1971 Capitol E-ST 571

Live In Paris
August 1971 Liberty LBS 83468

What You Hear Is What You Get
September 1971 UA UAD 60005/6

'Nuff Said
March 1972 UA UAS 29256

Feel Good
June 1972 UA UAS 29377

The Ike and Tina Turner Revue
December 1972 New World NW 6006

Let Me Touch Your Mind
February 1973 UA UAS 29423

Ike and Tina's Greatest Hits
(re-issue) February 1973 Warner K 36001

16 Peaches
May 1973 Mojo 2916 020

Outta Season
(re-issue) September 1973 Sunset SLS 51314

The World of Ike and Tina Turner
October 1973 UA UAD 60043/4

Nutbush City Limits
November 1973 UA UAS 29557

Tina Turner Country
October 1974 UA UAS 29572

Sweet Rhode Island Red
October 1974 UA UAS 29681

River Deep Mountain High
(re-issue) 1974 Mayfair AMLB 1021

River Deep Mountain High
(re-issue) 1975 Hamlet AMLP 8013

Tommy (soundtrack) *Acid Queen*
March 1975 Polydor 2657 014

Star Collection
March 1976 WEA Midi 36013

16 Great Performances
April 1975 ABC ABCL 5123

Her Man His Woman
(re-issue) April 1976 Vine VMP 1013

Souled From The Vaults
October 1975 DJM DJMD 8006

The Very Best of Ike and Tina
May 1976 UA UAS 29948

Souled From The Vaults
(re-issue) November 1976 DJM DJD 28006

Delila's Power
March 1977 UA UAS 30040

Soul Sellers
November 1979 Liberty LBR 1002

River Deep Mountain High
(re-issue) December 1979 MFP 50443

Juke Box Giants
November 1981 Audio Fidelity AFEMP 1021

Too Hot To Hold
January 1982 (cassette) Orchid ORC 001

Souled From The Vaults
(re-issue) April 1982 Audio Fidelity
AFESD 1038

Rock Me Baby
September 1982 Bulldog BDL 1045

Nice And Rough
March 1984 Liberty LBR 2600211
The Soul of Ike and Tina
April 1984 Kent 014
River Deep Mountain High
May 1984 Spot SPR 8548
Tough Enough
September 1984 Liberty EG 2602511

Tina Turner Singles

The Acid Queen/Rockin' And Rollin'
January 1976 UA UP 36043
*Root Toot Undisputable Rock'n'Roller/Fire
Down Below*
February 1979 UA UP 36485
*Sometimes When We Touch/Earthquake And
Hurricane*
April 1979 UA UP 36513
Backstabbers/Sunset On Sunset
November 1979 UA BP 322
Ball Of Confusion/Instrumental
Tina with BEF May 1982 Virgin VS 500
Let's Stay Together/I Wrote A Letter
November 1983 Capitol CL 316
Help/Rock'n'Roll Widow
February 1984 Capitol CL 325
*What's Love Got To Do With It/Don't Rush
Good Things*
June 1984 Capitol CL 334
Better Be Good To Me/When I Was Young
September 1984 Capitol CL 338
Private Dancer/Nutbush City Limits (live version)
December 1984 Capitol CL 343
I Can't Stand The Rain/Let's Pretend We're Married
1985 Capitol CL 352
*We Don't Need Another Hero
(Thunderdome) instrumental version*
July 1985 Capitol CL 364
One Of The Living/One Of The Living (dub
version)
September 1985 Capitol CL 376

Addicted To Love
March 1988 Capitol CDCL 484
The Best
August 1989 Capitol CDCL 543
I Don't Wanna Lose You
October 1989 Capitol CDCL 553
Look Me In The Heart
August 1990 EMI CDCLX 584
Be Tender With Me Baby

October 1990 Capitol CDCL 593
It Takes Two (Tina Turner with Rod Stewart)
November 1990 WEA ROD 1CD
Nutbush City Limits (90's version)
October 1991 Capitol CDCL 630
Way Of The World
October 1991 Capitol CDCL 637
Love Thing
January 1992 Capitol CDCL 644
I Want You Near Me
June 1992 Capitol CDCLS 659
I Don't Wanna Fight
May 1993 EMI CDRS 6346
Why Must We Wait Until Tonight?
June 1993 Parlophone CDRS 6366

Tina Turner Albums

Acid Queen
October 1975 UA UAS 29875
Rough
March 1979 UA UAG 30211
Love Explosion
September 1979 UA UAG 30267
Private Dancer
June 1984 Capitol Tina 1

Break Every Rule
September 1986 Capitol CDP 746 323 2
Live In Europe: Tina Turner
March 1988 Capitol CD ESTD 1
Foreign Affair
September 1989 Capitol CDESTU 2103
Rough
October 1990 Parlophone CZ 357
Love Explosion
October 1990 Parlophone CZ 358
Tina Turner Boxed Set
October 1990 Capitol CDP 795 246 2
Tina Turner Goes Country
February 1991 Connoisseur Collection
NSPCD 501
Simply The Best
October 1991 Capitol CDESTV 1
Acid Queen
October 1991 Fame CDFA 3141
What's Love Got To Do With It
June 1993 Parlophone EMI CDPSCD 128